What people are saying about *The Trellis and the Vine*

What Col and Tony have described here is exactly what I've been trying to do in my own life and in our congregation for years. According to this book, Christians are to be disciple-making disciples and pastors are to be trainers. Superb! This book sets out a crucial shift that is needed in the mindset of many pastors. The authors have carefully listened to the Bible. And they've worked on this book. The result is a book that is well-written and well-illustrated, but even more, a book that is full of biblical wisdom and practical advice. This is the best book I've read on the nature of church ministry.

Mark Dever
Senior Pastor, Capitol Hill Baptist Church, Washington DC, USA

I am thrilled that this book has been written! What God has done in Sydney over the last few decades is nothing less than supernatural—and we in South Africa have long been the beneficiaries. The model of ministry presented in this book has left an indelible mark on my own ministry and been of inestimable value to the denomination I belong to. The mindsets put forth in this book have not only impacted many of our churches, but have changed our regional thinking, planning and strategy. We are indebted to Col and Tony for putting into words a culture of ministry that is biblically pragmatic, deeply theological and, above all, passionately concerned for the lost.

Grant Retief
Rector, Christ Church, Umhlanga, South Africa

This is a simple, beautiful book that I plan to have every pastor and elder at The Village Church read. It quietly and calmly beckons us back to biblical, hands-on shepherding and is a book desperately needed among large churches in the West.

Matt Chandler
Lead Pastor, The Village Church, Dallas, Texas, USA

Gospel ministry is about God's glory and God's people! This excellent book takes us right to the heart of authentic Christian ministry. Any church will benefit hugely from studying and acting on it.

William Taylor
Rector, St Helen's Bishopsgate, London, UK

For over twenty years, I have seen the ideas in this excellent book developed, tested and improved in the active ministry of the gospel. They are the kind of counter-intuitive ideas that, once encountered and embraced, make you wonder why you did not always think this way.

Phillip D. Jensen
Dean of Sydney, St Andrew's Cathedral, Sydney, Australia

If I could put only one new book into the hands of every person preparing for ministry today, *The Trellis and the Vine* would be it. Marshall and Payne leverage decades of experience in one of the world's great cities with the hope of stimulating gospel growth around the globe. This book will also refresh every pastor who has ever asked, "What in the world am I *supposed* to be doing?" I came away energized, strengthened in my core calling and better prepared to bear fruit for Christ. In fact, it's so good that I want every leader and pastoral intern in our church to read it!

David Helm
Pastor, Holy Trinity Church, Chicago, Illinois, USA

It is impossible to read *The Trellis and the Vine* without having your cherished ministry assumptions profoundly challenged.

In your hands is a God-glorifying, scripturally-soaked re-evaluation of Christian ministry. It will untangle the anomaly of being a Christian without a radical missionary heart. It will identify the plethora of ministry structures that owe more to cultural pragmatism than the Bible. And above all, it will inspire us to serve the church of God, which he obtained with his own blood.

Richard Chin
National Director, Australian Fellowship of Evangelical Students, Sydney, Australia

God makes ministers in the midst of his church. It is in the context of the faithful local church that ministers are best taught, shaped and equipped. *The Trellis and the Vine* is a superb guide to preparing pastors and ministers for Christ's church. It comes from a ministry so deeply committed to the recovery of biblical truth and the cause of the gospel. The wisdom in this little book is invaluable. My advice: Keep a good stack on hand at all times, and put this book to good use.

R. Albert Mohler, Jr.
President, The Southern Baptist Theological Seminary, Louisville, Kentucky, USA

This book empathizes with the confusion that many pastors have when they allow themselves to lose focus on Jesus' goal for ministry, namely, to make disciple-makers. But it doesn't leave the pastor there in the cloud of desperation; it gives him the courage to trust in his Master's strategy again. And take courage: Jesus' strategy was able to reach countries as far as my own.

Cristóbal Cerón
General Coordinator, Gimnasio (MTS), Chile

There is no need greater (in the happy resurgence of robust, gospel-centred churches in the English-speaking world) than for us to think biblically and wisely about how we live and minister together in our congregations. All manner of folk are offering us their opinions as to how we ought to do this in this reforming era (in which some, if not many, rightly see the weaknesses of the ministry and methodology of the last fifty years, but whose prescriptions for remedy fall short of the standards of Scripture and wisdom). Yes, let's rethink what we are to do and be together as the church, but let's do it biblically, and with the wisdom of biblical discernment and pastoral experience. So I announce with joy that I have new conversation partners as I am asking myself, under the authority of God and Scripture, questions about the structure and ministry of my congregation: "Why are we doing what we are doing? Are we focusing on the right things? Is the gospel central? Are we making disciples? Has 'administry' trumped ministry? Is our corporate life and mission biblically shaped?" And more. As I ask these things, I am so deeply helped and heartened and humbled and corrected by the fidelity and wisdom of Colin Marshall and Tony Payne's profound little book that I can't but commend it to you.

Ligon Duncan
Senior Minister, First Presbyterian Church, Jackson, Mississippi, USA
(Past Moderator, General Assembly, Presbyterian Church in America)

The Trellis and the Vine is a must-read for every minister of the gospel. The principles in this book will revolutionize the way many of us do ministry, and help us to encourage and grow the next generation of gospel workers. So often we are caught up in building and maintaining our 'trellis' (ministry structure), and we forget that Christian ministry is all about the 'vine'—the people. Thank you for this clear, Bible-centred approach to the most important task in the world.

Ainsley Poulos
Equip Women Ministries, Sydney, Australia

This book is the perfect example of good theology driving practice. Col's many years of experience in recruiting and training pastors shines through on every page. Scattered with helpful personal examples, this book is a crucial read for people seeking to grapple with the biblical principles of gospel growth.

Paul Dale
Senior Pastor, Church by the Bridge, Sydney, Australia

The Trellis and the Vine is a dangerous book to read. It demolishes precious and much-loved idols like these: "If we just have the right vision and mission statement, they will come... If we just have the right vibe, they will come... If we just have the right speaker... the right band... the right building..."

The Trellis and the Vine reminds the church that Jesus says the exact opposite. Jesus tells us to be great commission-aries and to "Go... make disciples of all nations". *The Trellis and the Vine* is the best book I have read about mobilizing all Christians to be great commission-aries. It will turn church-shoppers into servants, and disciples into disciple-makers.

Ben Pfahlert
Director, Ministry Training Strategy (MTS), Sydney, Australia

This stimulating new book on *biblical* training will challenge some cherished methodologies. Tony and Col, though, are able to unsettle and critique with sympathy and understanding. Their observations are always judicious and never judgemental. Every page pulsates with a desire for the growth of the gospel and the maturing of the church. This is not the work of quick-fix pragmatists or armchair theologians, but the product of thirty years of effective ministry practice and reflection. It deserves to be widely read and discussed by all who are serious about every-person ministry in the church. It will be a set text at BCV!

Michael Raiter
Principal, The Bible College of Victoria, Melbourne, Australia

This book identifies vital change in culture, priority, energy, creativity, vision and ministry that we need today. This kind of change is hard work, and this book will help. The basic priorities in a local church will be the greatest influence on a person's future ministry, which is why this book is of strategic value. William Carey's influential 1792 *Enquiry* was about creating a useful trellis, but as a means, not an end in itself. Big minds keep focused on ends, not means, and significant ministries keep working on the vine. Praise God for this book.

Peter Adam
Principal, Ridley Melbourne Mission and Ministry College, Australia

About the authors

Colin Marshall has spent the past 30 years training men and women in the ministry of the gospel, both in university and local church contexts. He is a graduate of Moore Theological College (BTh, MA) and the author of *Growth Groups*, a training course for small group leaders, and *Passing the Baton*, a handbook for ministry apprenticeship. Until 2006 he directed the Ministry Training Strategy, and is now heading up Vinegrowers, a new training ministry aiming to help pastors and other ministry leaders implement the principles in this book (see **vinegrowers.com**).

Tony Payne has spent more than 20 years in Christian writing and editing as the Publishing Director of Matthias Media. He is a graduate of Moore Theological College (BTh Hons), and the author or co-author of many popular books and resources, including *Two Ways to Live: The choice we all face*, *Fatherhood: What it is and what it's for*, *Guidance and the Voice of God*, *Prayer and the Voice of God*, *Six Steps to Reading Your Bible* and *The Course of Your Life*.

THE TRELLIS AND THE VINE

THE MINISTRY MIND-SHIFT THAT CHANGES EVERYTHING

COLIN MARSHALL
AND TONY PAYNE

The Trellis and the Vine
© Matthias Media 2009

Matthias Media
(St Matthias Press Ltd ACN 067 558 365)
PO Box 225
Kingsford NSW 2032
Australia
Telephone: (02) 9233 4627; international: +61 2 9233 4627
Email: info@matthiasmedia.com.au
Internet: www.matthiasmedia.com.au

Matthias Media (USA)
Telephone: 330 953 1702; international: +1 330 953 1702
Email: sales@matthiasmedia.com
Internet: www.matthiasmedia.com

ISBN 978 1 921441 58 5

Cover design and typesetting by Lankshear Design.

Contents

Acknowledgements

Col and I have been writing this book, often without realizing it, for most of the past 25 years. It's how we've come to think about Christian ministry, and it has driven and shaped what we have spent our lives doing. In Col's case, that has meant founding and directing a training organization devoted to raising up workers for the gospel—the Ministry Training Strategy (MTS); for me, it has meant founding and directing a publishing ministry focused on producing resources to facilitate gospel ministry—Matthias Media.

The army of friends, family, colleagues and partners who have taught us, shaped us and supported us over those years is impossible to list in this brief space. None of it would have happened without the extraordinary influence and friendship of Phillip Jensen, who has been there all along, who taught and shaped us profoundly, and who was instrumental in forming both MTS and Matthias Media. It's also impossible to imagine us getting to the point of writing this book without the friendship, support and hard work of Ian Carmichael, Marty Sweeney, Archie Poulos, Paddy Benn, John Dykes, Simon Pillar, Laurie Scandrett, Robert Tong, Tony Willis, David Glinatsis, Kathryn Thompson, John McConville, Hans Norved, Ben Pfahlert, and a long list of others. Many of these friends have worked hard to provide the trellis for our vine. A special thanks also goes to Gordon Cheng, who laboured long and hard to help bring this project to fruition.

While we're acknowledging the friends and partners who

shaped this book, I also want to emphasize that this is Col's book more than it is mine. We talk a lot in the pages that follow about working closely with people, discipling them, helping them to grow and flourish in ministry, and sticking with them over the long haul. Col has done that with me over the past 30-odd years. And although I'm now privileged to work alongside Col as a brother and colleague (and I know he is very grateful for all the 'word-smithing' I've done), I want to make clear that most of the ideas that follow are now mine because they were first his.

Finally, we want to thank our families, and particularly the godly wives God has blessed us with: Col's Jacquie and my Ali. Their love and encouragement and words and example mean more than we can say.

TP, August 2009.

Chapter 1

The trellis and the vine

We have two trellises in our backyard.

The one attached to the back wall of the garage is a very fine piece of latticework. I wish I could claim it as my own creation, but I cannot. It is sturdy and dependable and neatly designed, and the federation-green paintwork has been kept fresh. It lacks only one thing: a vine.

I imagine there once was a vine, unless the construction of the trellis was one of those handyman tasks that took so long that, in the end, no-one got around to planting something to grow on it. Someone certainly put a lot of time and care into building it. It's almost a work of art. But if there was ever a vine that laced itself around this beautiful trellis, there is now no trace of it.

The other trellis leans up against the side fence and is barely visible beneath a flourishing jasmine vine. With some fertilizer and an occasional watering, the jasmine keeps thrusting out new shoots, winding its way across, up and over the fence, putting out its delicate white flowers as the warmth of spring approaches. Some pruning is needed every now and then, and some weeding around the base. I've also had to spray it once or twice to stop caterpillars from feasting on the juicy green leaves. But the jasmine just keeps growing.

It's hard to tell what condition the trellis is in under the jasmine, but at the few points where it is still visible, I can see that it hasn't been painted in a long time. At one end, it has been prised off the fence by the insistent fingers of the jasmine, and although I have tried to re-attach it more than once, it is useless. The jasmine has taken over. I know I will have to do something about this in the long term, because eventually the weight of the jasmine will pull the trellis off the fence altogether and the whole thing will collapse.

I have often thought of taking a cutting from the jasmine and seeing if it will grow on the beautiful but vacant trellis on the garage, although it almost seems a shame to cover it up.

How trellis work takes over

As I have sat on my back verandah and observed the two trellises, it has occurred to me more than once that most churches are a mixture of trellis and vine. The basic work of any Christian ministry is to preach the gospel of Jesus Christ in the power of God's Spirit, and to see people converted, changed and grow to maturity in that gospel. That's the work of planting, watering, fertilizing and tending the vine.

However, just as some sort of framework is needed to help a vine grow, so Christian ministries also need some structure and support. It may not be much, but at the very least we need somewhere to meet, some Bibles to read from, and some basic structures of leadership within our group. All Christian churches, fellowships or ministries have some kind of trellis that gives shape and support to the work. As the ministry grows, the trellis also needs attention. Management, finances, infrastructure, organization, governance—these all become more important and more complex as the vine grows. In this sense, good trellis workers are invaluable, and all growing ministries need them.

What's the state of the trellis and the vine at your church?

Perhaps trellis work has taken over from vine work. There are committees, structures, programs, activities and fundraising efforts, and many people put lots of time into keeping them all going, but the actual work of growing the vine falls to a very few. In fact, perhaps the only time real vine-growing work happens is in the regular Sunday service, and then only by the pastor as he preaches his sermon.

If this is your church, then there's every chance the vine is looking a bit tired. The leaves are less green, the flowers are less profuse, and it has been some time since any new shoots have been seen. The pastor keeps working away manfully, feeling overworked, under-appreciated and a little discouraged that his faithful vine work each Sunday doesn't seem to bear much fruit. In fact, he often feels he would like to do more to help and encourage others to be involved in vine work, the work of watering and planting and helping people to grow in Christ. But the sad truth is that most of the trellis work also seems to fall to him to organize—rosters, property and building issues, committees, finances, budgets, overseeing the church office, planning and running events. There's just no time.

And that's the thing about trellis work: it tends to take over from vine work. Perhaps it's because trellis work is easier and less personally threatening. Vine work is personal and requires much prayer. It requires us to depend on God, and to open our mouths and speak God's word in some way to another person. By nature (by sinful nature, that is) we shy away from this. What would you rather do: go to a church working bee and sweep up some leaves, or share the gospel with your neighbour over the back fence? Which is easier: to have a business meeting about the state of the carpet, or to have a difficult personal meeting where you need to rebuke a friend about his sinful behaviour?

Trellis work also often looks more impressive than vine work. It's more visible and structural. We can point to something tangible—a committee, an event, a program, a budget, an infrastructure—and say that we have achieved something. We can build our trellis till it reaches to the heavens, in the hope of making a name for ourselves, but there may still be very little growth in the vine.

The concentration on trellis work that is so common in many churches derives from an institutional view of Christian ministry. It is very possible for churches, Christian organizations and whole denominations to be given over totally to maintaining their institution. One church I know of has 23 different organizations and structures functioning weekly, all of which are listed on the weekly bulletin. All of these different activities started as good ideas for growth in church life at some point in the past, and they certainly result in lots of people being around the church building during the week doing lots of things. But how much actual vine work is taking place? How many people are hearing God's word and by the power of his Spirit growing in knowledge and godliness? In this particular church, the answer is very few.

Whatever the reason, there is no doubt that in many churches, maintaining and improving the trellis constantly takes over from tending the vine. We run meetings, maintain buildings, sit on committees, appoint and look after staff, do administration, raise money, and generally tick the boxes that our denomination wants ticked.

Somehow, this tends to happen particularly as we get older. We start to tire of vine work, and take on more and more organizational responsibilities. Sometimes this may even be because we are perceived to be successful vine-growers, and so we get out of vine-growing and into telling other people about vine-growing.

But it's even worse than that when we pause to consider the commission that God has given all of us as his people. The parable of the trellis and the vine is not just a picture of the struggles of my own local church; it's also a picture of the progress of the gospel in my street and suburb and city and world.

The vine and the commission

In 1792, a young man named William Carey published a booklet entitled *An Enquiry into the Obligations of Christians to use Means for the Conversion of the Heathen*. In it, Carey argued *against* the prevailing view of the time that the Great Commission of Matthew 28 had been fulfilled by the first apostles and was not applicable to the church in succeeding generations. For Carey, this was an abdication of our responsibility. He saw the Great Commission as a duty and privilege for all generations, and thus began the modern missionary movement.

For most of us, this is no longer controversial. Of course we should be sending out missionaries to the ends of the earth and seeking to reach the whole world for Christ. But is that really what Matthew 28 is calling upon us to do? Does the commission also apply to our own church, and to each Christian disciple? These famous verses are worth a closer look.

When the slightly overwhelmed disciples saw the risen Jesus on the mountain in Galilee, they fell down before him with a mixture of awe and doubt in their hearts. And when Jesus came and spoke to them, his words would have done nothing to calm them down.

"All authority in heaven and on earth has been given to me", he tells them (Matt 28:18). This astonishing claim has overtones of Daniel 7 about it. When "one like a son of man" comes into the presence of the Ancient of Days in Daniel 7, he is given "dominion and glory and a kingdom, that all peoples, nations, and languages should serve him" (Dan 7:13-14).

"This is who I am", Jesus is telling his disciples. And for the past three years, the disciples have seen it for themselves. Jesus has walked among them as the powerful Son of Man, healing the sick, raising the dead, teaching with authority, forgiving sins, and saying things like this:

> "When the Son of Man comes in his glory, and all the angels with him, then he will sit on his glorious throne. Before him will be gathered all the nations, and he will separate people one from another as a shepherd separates the sheep from the goats." (Matt 25:31-32)

And now, in the presence of the Son of Man on the hillside in Galilee, they are seeing the fulfilment of Daniel's vision. Here is the Man before whom all peoples, from every nation and tongue, will bow.

It is on this basis—the unique, supreme and worldwide authority of the risen Son of Man—that Jesus commissions his disciples to make disciples of all nations. Sometimes our translations may give the impression that 'go' is the emphasis of the command, but the main verb of the sentence is 'make disciples', with three subordinate participles hanging off it: going (or 'as you go'), baptizing and teaching.

'Baptizing' and 'teaching' are the means by which the disciples are to be made. Whatever else baptism might symbolize or involve, here it refers to the initiation of disciples into repentance and submission to the authoritative Jesus, the reigning Lord of the world.

The 'teaching' that the disciples are to do reproduces what Jesus himself has done with them. He has been their 'teacher' (cf. Matt 12:38; 19:16; 22:16, 24, 36; 26:18), and as Jesus has taught them they have grown in knowledge and understanding. The disciples are now, in turn, to make new disciples by teaching them to obey everything commanded by their Master. This 'making-disciples-by-teaching' corresponds to preaching the gospel in the parallel mission mandate in Luke, where Jesus says "repentance and forgiveness of sins should be proclaimed in his name to all nations, beginning from Jerusalem" (Luke 24:47).

But what about the 'going'? Traditionally (or at least after Carey), this has been read as a missionary mandate, a charter for sending out gospel workers to the world. However, this can lead local churches to think that they are obeying the Great Commission if they send money (and missionaries) overseas. But the emphasis of the sentence is not on 'going'. The main verb is "make disciples", and the 'going' is a participle indicating a necessary accompanying action (i.e. that the disciples will have to 'go' from where they are with Jesus on the mountain in Galilee in order to make disciples). The commission is not fundamentally about mission out there somewhere else in another country. *It's a commission that makes disciple-making the normal agenda and priority of every church and every Christian disciple.*

The authority of Jesus is not limited in any respect. He is the Lord and Master of my street, my neighbours, my suburb, my workmates, my family, my city, my nation—and yes, the whole world. We would not ever want to stop sending out missionaries to preach the gospel in places where it is yet to be heard, but we must also see disciple-making as our central task in our homes and neighbourhoods and churches.

Jesus' instruction to "make disciples" in Matthew 28:19 is not just a specific word to the apostles gathered around him at the time of his final resurrection appearance. The first disciples were instructed to "make disciples" of others. And because these newly-made disciples were under the universal lordship of Christ, and were to obey everything that Jesus had taught, they fell under exactly the same obligation as the original twelve to get on with the job of announcing the lordship of Christ; as did their hearers, and so on "to the end of the age".

Don Carson concludes that "the injunction is given at least to the Eleven, but to the Eleven in their own role as disciples (v. 16). Therefore they are paradigms for all disciples... It is binding on

all Jesus' disciples to make others what they themselves are—
disciples of Jesus Christ."[1]

To be a disciple is to be called to make new disciples.
Of course, Christians will receive and exercise differing gifts
and ministries (more on this in the chapters that follow). But
because all are disciples of Christ, standing in relation to him as
teacher and pupil, master and follower, all are disciple-makers.

Thus the goal of Christian ministry is quite simple, and in
a sense measurable: are we making and nurturing genuine
disciples of Christ? The church always tends towards
institutionalism and secularization. The focus shifts to
preserving traditional programs and structures, and the goal of
discipleship is lost. The mandate of disciple-making provides
the touchstone for whether our church is engaging in Christ's
mission. Are we making genuine disciples of Jesus Christ? Our
goal is not to make church members or members of our
institution, but genuine disciples of Jesus.

Or to return to our parable—our goal is to grow the vine,
not the trellis.

THE IMAGE OF THE TRELLIS AND THE VINE RAISES ALL THE
fundamental questions of Christian ministry:

- What is the vine for?
- How does the vine grow?
- How does the vine relate to my church?
- What is vine work and what is trellis work, and how can
  we tell the difference?
- What part do different people play in growing the vine?
- How can we get more people involved in vine work?
- What is the right relationship between the trellis and the
  vine?

In the following chapters, we will be suggesting that there is an urgent need to answer these questions afresh. Confusion reigns. Everyone wants their churches to grow, but most are unsure how and where to start. Church growth gurus come and go. Ministry methods fall in and out of favour like women's fashion. We troop from one new technique to the next, hoping that this one (at last!) may be the secret to success.

Even among those godly, faithful pastors who avoid the trendsetting fads of Christian marketing, there is confusion—most especially between what Christian ministry is in the Bible, and what Christian ministry has become in the particular tradition or denomination of which they are part. We are all captive to our traditions and influenced by them more than we realize. And the effect of tradition and long practice is not always that some terrible error becomes entrenched; more often it is that our focus shifts away from our main task and agenda, which is disciple-making. We become so used to doing things one way (often for good reason at first) that important elements are neglected and forgotten, to our cost. We become imbalanced, and then wonder why we go in circles.

Endnote
1. DA Carson, 'Matthew' in Frank E Gaebelein (ed.), *The Expositor's Bible Commentary*, vol. 8, Zondervan, Grand Rapids, 1984, p. 596.

Chapter 2

Ministry mind-shifts

Over the course of this book, we are going to suggest that most Christian churches today need to undertake a radical re-evaluation of what Christian ministry really is—what its aims and goals are, how it proceeds, and what part we all play in its exercise. In the chapters that follow (particularly chapters 3-5), we will be digging into the Scriptures to lay the foundations for this re-think, and to argue for its necessity and urgency.

However, before we make the argument in detail, we thought it would be worth providing a glimpse of where we're heading. We will be arguing that structures don't grow ministry any more than trellises grow vines, and that most churches need to make a conscious shift—away from erecting and maintaining structures, and towards *growing people who are disciple-making disciples of Christ.*

This may require some radical, and possibly painful, changes of mindset. Here are some examples of the mental shifts we might need to make. Each of them touches on a different aspect of structural thinking that inhibits people ministry. Once we make the transition, however, this will open up new vistas for ministry and ministry training.

1. From running programs to building people
When planning ministry for the year ahead, there are two

broad approaches we could adopt. One is to consider existing church programs (such as Sunday meetings, youth work, children's ministry and Bible study groups) and then work out how such programs can be maintained and improved. The other approach is to start with the people in your church, having no particular structures or programs in mind, and then consider who are these people God has given you, how you can help them grow in Christian maturity, and what form their gifts and opportunities might take.

This is a revolutionary mind-shift: when we think about our people, it moves our focus to putting them first and building ministries around them. In the course of doing so, it may become apparent that some programs no longer serve any worthwhile purpose. It may also become apparent that a program is no longer viable because the people who once made it work are no longer available. So the program can be done away with. This might be painful for those attached to them (it takes guts to shoot a dead horse!), but new ministries will begin to arise as you train members of your congregation to use their various gifts and opportunities.

2. From running events to training people

Churches typically adopt an 'event-based' approach to evangelism. They use a variety of events to proclaim the gospel: church meetings, guest services, mission meetings, men's breakfasts, women's suppers, and many other creative gatherings. In order to appear successful, they keep on running more and more of these events.

However, at one level, this tactic is failing. In our post-Christian, secular age, most unbelievers will never come to our events. Even our members are patchy in their attendance. The 'event' tactic relies partly on the appeal and gifts of a guest speaker, and this means we're limited by the availability of such people in what we can run. For the church pastor, and for key lay people, setting up and running events can end up dominating life, with all our time being spent on getting people to come along to things. Yet, despite the work they involve, in some respects events are a centralizing tactic: they're convenient and easy to control for the leader/organizer, but they require unbelievers to come to us on our own terms. In the end, an 'event approach' distracts us from both training and evangelism.

If we want our strategy to be people-focused, we should concentrate on *training*, which increases the number and effectiveness of gospel communicators (i.e. people who can speak the good news both in personal conversations and in public settings). This sort of strategy involves identifying and equipping more speakers, thereby increasing the number, variety and effectiveness of events. In addition, you can use events to train your workers. If all the members of your congregation are given the opportunity to be trained in evangelism, more unbelievers will attend our events.

But please note: this is a chaotic strategy—an inconvenient strategy. It takes time to train evangelists. It takes time for young evangelists to build their own ministries as they go about preaching the word. It will mean we will have to relinquish control of our programs for, as the gospel is preached, Christ will gather his people into all kinds of fellowships that may or may not fit into our neat structures.

3. From using people to growing people

Volunteers are the ones who maintain and expand church programs. Under God, volunteers are the lifeblood of our churches: they pour their evenings and weekends into Sunday meetings, children's work, youth group, Bible studies, committees, looking after church property, and so on. The danger of having such willing volunteers is that we use them, exploit them and forget to train them. Then they burn out, their ministry is curtailed, and we find that we have failed to develop their Christian life and ministry potential. Instead of using our volunteers, we should consider how we can encourage them and help them grow in the knowledge and love of Christ, because service flows from Christian growth and not growth from service.

For example, one committed, keen couple I know served faithfully as Bible study leaders for six consecutive years, while also juggling significant study and work commitments. In the seventh year, with the encouragement of their pastor, they took a 'sabbatical'—a break from leading Bible study to refresh themselves; to simply belong to a group and recharge their batteries. After their year off, they plunged back into leadership again.

We need to care for people and help them to flourish and grow in ministry, not squeeze them dry in the interests of keeping our programs running.

4. From filling gaps to training new workers

One of the immediate pressures upon ministers is to fill gaps left by leaders who leave our programs. But if we just focus on gap filling, we'll never move out of maintenance mode: we're just keeping existing ministries afloat instead of branching out into new ones.

We should start with the people that God has given us, not our programs. We need to consider each person as a gift from Christ to our congregation, and equip them for ministry accordingly. So instead of thinking, "Who can fill this gap in our personnel?", perhaps the question we need to consider is "What ministry could this member exercise?"

We could recount many examples from our own experience of where this has and hasn't happened. Take Sarah, for example, an elite sportswoman converted as an adult through sports ministry. Sarah was well followed-up and established in her faith, and her church provided a strong and edifying environment. What's more, Sarah had a passion for Christ and for evangelism, and had a large network of non-Christian friends, teammates and acquaintances with whom to share the gospel. However, instead of training and encouraging Sarah to pursue this evangelistic ministry, the church strongly urged her to become a member of the church management committee, because there was a gap and a need, and Sarah was enthusiastic and willing to help. The church was gap-filling, not building ministry around the gifts and opportunities of people.

A more positive example was Dave, a young man who suffered from schizophrenia. Dave was a very intelligent and able person who loved the Lord, but his illness meant that nearly every common avenue for ministry was closed to him. He didn't have the mental stability or strength to lead Bible studies or follow up new Christians or contribute to other church events or programs. However, in his lucid and rational periods, Dave had enormous potential for evangelism and ministry among his many friends and contacts who also suffered from mental or emotional disorders. His pastor trained and encouraged Dave in this ministry, and had other Christian friends support him, back him up, and help him with follow-up. It was a marvellous instance of seeing the ministry potential of a unique person, and helping and equipping him to make disciples.

If we begin viewing things in these terms, it will open up new areas of ministry centred on the particular gifts and opportunities of our members. Instead of filling a vacancy on a committee, one of our members might start a ministry to his/her ethnic community, or a Bible study group in his/her workplace. Furthermore, focusing on people will help us to discover and train potential candidates for full-time word ministry (more on this in chapters 9 and 10).

5. From solving problems to helping people make progress

A common feeling among Christians is that they only get prayed for and visited when they're sick or out of work. Of course, our churches will always contain people with problems; God's people have many needs, just like the rest of the population. And as ministers of Christ, we need to love and welcome everyone, whatever their individual needs and situations, and not dismiss their problems with cheap words (Jas 2:14-17).

However, we don't want to create the kind of ministry environment where the only way people can relate to one another is by discussing their problems. If ministry in our churches is based on reacting to the problems people raise, many will receive no attention because they are more reserved in sharing their problems. The goal is to move people forward in holy living and knowledge of God, whether they are facing problems or not; this is why we proclaim Christ, "warning everyone and teaching everyone with all wisdom, that we may present everyone mature in Christ" (Col 1:28).

So ask yourself whether your ministries are reactive or proactive. If you are mostly reacting to people's problems, you won't have the energy to put into proactive training and growing new work. If you take a problem approach to ministry, people with the most critical needs will dominate your programs, and these needs will wear you out and exhaust you, and reduce the effectiveness of your other ministries.

6. From clinging to ordained ministry to developing team leadership

Denominations are quite right to ordain or accredit ministers to be faithful shepherds of Christ's flock. However, there are a number of ways in which the practice of ordination hinders ministry training in churches. Firstly, if the only 'real' ministers are people ordained by the denomination, our churches will not have any incentive to encourage others who are not ordained to test their gifts of preaching and teaching. Secondly, if the policy is limited to filling ministerial gaps in vacant churches, why look for evangelists and church-planters who could grow new work? Thirdly, we will tend to select people for training who fit the mould of the ordained minister, ignoring the fact that some gifted people may not fit comfortably in traditional ministries, and that their gifts could potentially lead them to break new ground for the gospel outside existing denominational structures.

In traditional thinking, the ordained minister of a church is expected to exercise all the public ministries of word and sacrament, pastoral visiting, evangelism, school Scripture classes and more. But if we are going to focus on training, this implies team ministry. Church members are often opposed to team ministry for a variety of reasons. Firstly, training appears elitist as only the few are selected. Secondly, some Christians only want the 'real' minister to preach or visit, and are not happy when his place is taken by a trainee or lay minister. Finally, the time that the minister spends training the team is often perceived as a distraction from his pastoral duties. However, the benefits of team ministry are many, so it's well worth freeing up our ministers so they have the time and space to build themselves a team.

7. From focusing on church polity to forging ministry partnerships

Issues concerning how churches are governed often dominate local ministry. At one level this is to be expected, because all denominations are partially defined by their distinctive understanding of church government, and it's important for a church to be faithful to its evangelical heritage. However, inflexible commitment to a particular polity can destroy training. Churches can find themselves spending too much time debating questions like "Where do trainee ministers and ministry teams fit into our structures? Are they elders, deacons, ministers or members of the church committee?" It's probably more helpful to think of these things in terms of ministry partnerships rather than political structures.

Another way to think about it is that elders and congregational leaders should be active vine-growers themselves before we consider giving them responsibility for oversight. They should be the kind of people who are reading the Bible one to one with others and sharing Christ with their neighbours.

8. From relying on training institutions to establishing local training

Bringing together gifted and scholarly pastors to provide rigorous theological and academic training in a college setting is a wise strategy. This sort of training is essential for both lay and ordained ministers. But a college cannot be expected to provide total training in the character, conviction and skill that is required for ministers and co-workers. Much of this ought to be done through training 'on the job' in church life. So it's ideal if education in colleges and training in churches can work together hand in hand. This may not always be possible concurrently. For example, in our part of the world it is common for formal theological education to be 'sandwiched' between a ministry apprenticeship before college and in-service practical training after college. (For more on local ministry apprenticeship, see chapter 11.)

There are also lots of opportunities for churches to integrate formal or external training into their regular training and growing of people—for example, participating in a distance education program to train lay people in theology alongside other training.

9. From focusing on immediate pressures to aiming for long-term expansion

We are easily consumed by keeping ministry programs running. The urgent crowds out the important, and everyone thinks that their agenda should be dealt with first. We know that training leaders will help to maintain and expand our ministries, but it takes all our energies just to keep the wheels turning. However, if we take our focus off our immediate pressures and aim for long-term expansion, the pressures we face will become less immediate and may eventually disappear.

10. From engaging in management to engaging in ministry

Ministers do need to be responsible managers of the resources entrusted to them, and therefore they will always have a certain amount of administration to do. But the trap for them is that they become so caught up in the management exercise, they weaken the ministry of teaching and training. How many hours per week does your minister spend attending committees, managing property, organizing programs or conducting church business? Could you train others to take over some of this work? Could your minister be relieved of some of his administrative workload so that he can devote time to training one or two new leaders?

11. From seeking church growth to desiring gospel growth

Once we've spent time and resources training our leaders, we soon fear losing them. However, one of our goals in training people should be to encourage some of them into further formal training in theology so that they might progress into denominational or missionary ministry. We must be exporters of trained people instead of hoarders of trained people. In a resource-poor church, this can be very hard to do. Even in churches with many leaders, regular turnover and re-training is demanding. But our view of gospel work must be global as well as local: the goal isn't church growth (in the sense of our local church expanding in numbers, budget, church-plants and reputation) but gospel growth. If we train and send workers into new fields (both local and global), our local ministry might not grow numerically but the gospel will advance through these new ministers of the word.

LET US TRY TO ILLUSTRATE WHAT THESE MIND-SHIFTS MEAN IN practice with just one nitty-gritty example.

Imagine a reasonably solid Christian said to you after church one Sunday morning, "Look, I'd like to get more involved here and make a contribution, but I just feel like there's nothing for me to do. I'm not on the 'inside'; I don't get asked to be on committees or lead Bible studies. What can I do?"

What would you immediately think or say? Would you start thinking of some event or program about to start that they could help with? Some job that needed doing? Some ministry that they could join or support?

This is how we are used to thinking about the involvement of church members in congregational life—in terms of jobs and roles: usher, Bible study leader, Sunday School teacher, treasurer, elder, musician, song leader, money counter, and so on. The implication of this way of thinking for congregation members is clear: if all the jobs and roles are taken, then there's really nothing for me to do in this church. I'm reduced to being a passenger. I'll just wait until I'm asked to 'do something'. The implication for the pastoral staff is similar: getting people involved and active means finding a job for them to do. In fact, the church growth gurus say that giving someone a job to do within the first six months of their joining your church is vital for them to feel like they belong.

However, if the real work of God is people work—the prayerful speaking of his word by one person to another—then the jobs are never all taken. The opportunities for Christians to minister personally to others are limitless.

So you could pause, and reply to your friend, "See that guy sitting over there on his own? That's Julie's husband. He's on the fringe of things here; in fact, I'm not really sure whether he's crossed the line yet and become a Christian. How about I introduce you to him, and you arrange to have breakfast with him once a fortnight and read the Bible together? Or see that couple over there? They are both fairly recently converted, and really in need of encouragement and mentoring. Why don't you and your wife have them over, get to know them, and read and pray together once a month? And if you still have time, and want to contribute some more, start praying for the people in your street, and then invite them all to a barbeque at your place. That's the first step towards talking with them about the gospel, or inviting them along to something."

Of course, there's every chance that the person will then say, "But I don't know how to do those things! I'm not sure I'd know what to say or where to start."

To which you reply, "Oh that's okay. Let's start meeting together, and I can train you."

Now if you're a pastor reading this book, your reaction at this point might be something like this: "Okay, right. Now I really know these guys are living in a dream. In their fantasy world, I'm supposed to have time to meet individually with all the members of my congregation, and personally train and mentor them so they can in turn personally minister to others. Have they seen my diary? Do they have *any* idea of the pressure I'm under? If that's what they mean by a mind-shift, it sounds more like a brain-explosion to me!"

Well, we haven't seen your diary, but if it's anything like most pastors' diaries, we know very well the pressure you're under. And in due course, we'll get to the nitty-gritty of how these sorts of mind-shifts play out in the day-to-day life of real churches.

However, there is some vital biblical work to be done first. To understand the scriptural foundations for re-focusing our ministries around people rather than structures, we have to go back and re-examine our core assumptions about what God is doing in our world, how he is doing it, who he is using to do it, and what it all means for Christian discipleship and ministry.

Chapter 3

What in the world is God doing?

In the quiet moments, when you're being honest with yourself and God, do the following thoughts ever pass through your mind?

God, what are you doing?!

We know that you are strong and mighty and majestic. You rule over everything. You hold the world in your hand.

But how long are you going to leave us like this?

We're begging you for some growth, for strength, for some *upside*. You know how it is. Numbers are stagnant, morale is flagging, the money is all over the place.

We're a joke. The world laughs at us.

Every mistake and scandal, real or imagined, is raked over with glee by the latte-sipping reptiles of the media—the ones with the trendy, thick-rimmed glasses and the 'correct' opinions.

Is it that you are angry with us? When are you going to do something to turn this around?

Because don't forget that the whole thing is your idea. You planted the vine in the first place—cleared the ground for it in the backyard, dug a hole, put up the

trellis—and we flourished. But now look at us! We're
being eaten alive.

Restore us, O Lord, God of hosts! Let your face shine
that we may be saved!

Apart from the last two sentences, which are a direct quote, the
rest of this little outburst is a re-phrasing of the 80th psalm,
which was written at a time when Israel felt like many
churches do today. The days of God's power and redemption
and victory all seemed to be in the past. More to the point, his
favour—the shining of his face upon them—was worryingly
absent. God seemed to them like a disappointed father who
had watched his wayward son embarrass and humiliate him
once too often, and now simply turned away, too appalled and
heartbroken to watch.

It's not so hard today to find these sorts of words in our
hearts and on our lips. Our churches falter and stumble. Growth
is slow, non-existent or (to use that wonderful modern
euphemism) 'negative'. We potter along in our ministries with
our enthusiasm waxing and waning, but the real action seems
always to be somewhere else—either in some other Christian
movement or in the world itself. Presidents and prime
ministers are elected, trophies are won and lost, TV dramas are
watched by millions. When 'all the news that's fit to print' is
carefully read, there is no mention of what is happening in our
little church. We are not news. When a couple walks past our
church on Sunday morning on their way to the park with their
dog, and hears the faint sounds of our singing, what do they
think? "Man, that place is where the action is!" One suspects
not. More likely they think, "Poor misguided souls" or "How
quaint!" or "I didn't think people did that any more" or some
other dismissive thought.

Modern churches (at least in the West) may not be under
the direct attack and disaster that Israel was experiencing, but

we certainly still wonder what God is doing in the world. Is he still listening? Is he going to act? I thought he was the Lord and Master of all—if so, what's the plan?!

Many of the psalms plumb these depths. But Psalm 80 has the distinction of exploring these ideas via the image of Israel as God's vine:

> Restore us, O God of hosts;
>> let your face shine, that we may be saved!
> You brought a vine out of Egypt;
>> you drove out the nations and planted it.
> You cleared the ground for it;
>> it took deep root and filled the land.
> The mountains were covered with its shade,
>> the mighty cedars with its branches.
> It sent out its branches to the sea
>> and its shoots to the River.
> Why then have you broken down its walls,
>> so that all who pass along the way pluck its fruit?
> The boar from the forest ravages it,
>> and all that move in the field feed on it. (Ps 80:7-13)

Here we find ourselves plunged into the middle of a story that has been unfolding since before there were any such things as vines, or for that matter earth into which they could be planted. It's the story of what God is really doing on planet earth. It begins with his plan to create all things by and for his Son, and it culminates in new heavens and a new earth, populated by a newly resurrected people of God who are united to Jesus Christ.

But here, in Psalm 80, it all hangs in the balance. After the wreckage of the Fall and the judgement of the Flood and Babel, God had planned to gather people from every nation to himself by carving out for himself one particular nation descended from Abraham: Israel. Over centuries, this plan had begun to unfold. The nation grew like a young vigorous plant and, despite the suffering of its slavery in Egypt, God rescued it, drove out nations before it, and planted it in the ground he had prepared.

Now the whole project was on the brink of ruin. The walls of the vineyard had been broken down, and all those who passed—including those with tusks and curly tails—were taking the chance to pluck the grapes. If we can extend the metaphor a little further, even the vine itself wasn't healthy. It was infected with disobedience, faithlessness and the worship of false gods.

It is at this low point in the history of God's plans that the psalmist cries out for mercy and rescue. It is also at this point that the prophets cry out with God's answer—that there will be judgement in the first place for Israel's sin, but that there is also the promise of mercy, rescue and restoration, in God's own time and way.

What the prophets did and didn't know

The prophets express these twin themes of judgement and mercy in many ways, but since we have started with the vine image, let us continue with it. Hosea condemned Israel as a luxuriant but ultimately false and doomed vine, but also prophesied that God would make the plant blossom once again:

> Israel is a luxuriant vine
> that yields its fruit.
> The more his fruit increased,
> the more altars he built;
> as his country improved,
> he improved his pillars.
> Their heart is false;
> now they must bear their guilt.

The LORD will break down their altars
　　and destroy their pillars. (Hos 10:1-2)

I will heal their apostasy;
　　I will love them freely,
　　for my anger has turned from them.
I will be like the dew to Israel;
　　he shall blossom like the lily;
　　he shall take root like the trees of Lebanon;
his shoots shall spread out;
　　his beauty shall be like the olive,
　　and his fragrance like Lebanon.
They shall return and dwell beneath my shadow;
　　they shall flourish like the grain;
they shall blossom like the vine;
　　their fame shall be like the wine of Lebanon.
　　(Hos 14:4-7)

It seemed to all outward appearances that nothing was going on except sin, failure and judgement. And yet the prophets promised that, like a phoenix from the ashes, Israel would rise again by the life-giving power of their God. The vine would blossom once more, and grow to be a beautiful plant known throughout the world. But the path to these glories would be through suffering and judgement. There was no avoiding the consequences of sin. Somehow, at some future time, God would bring his people through judgement and out the other side into the sunshine of his salvation.

All God's promises are 'yes' and 'amen' in Jesus Christ (2 Cor 1:20), and this one is no exception. The apostle Peter spoke of the fulfilment of the prophetic promise in his first letter to the descendants of Israel scattered throughout the ancient world, the "elect exiles of the dispersion". In one of the most glorious paragraphs in the whole New Testament, he wrote:

Concerning this salvation, the prophets who prophesied about the grace that was to be yours searched and inquired carefully, inquiring what person or time the Spirit of Christ in them was indicating when he predicted the sufferings of Christ and the subsequent glories. It was revealed to them that they were serving not themselves but you, in the things that have now been announced to you through those who preached the good news to you by the Holy Spirit sent from heaven, things into which angels long to look. (1 Pet 1:10-12)

Rarely has so much of the theological space-time continuum been packed into so few words. It starts with the prophets speaking of the gracious salvation that was to be revealed, and yet not being able to figure out exactly when and by whom the salvation would come. It ends with angels longing to gaze into the extraordinary fulfilment of the prophetic promise.

What the prophets did know was that the path to glory would be via the sufferings of God's Christ—which is exactly what you would expect when you think about it. God's message to Israel throughout the prophets was always this: you will suffer deeply because of sin, but glory and restoration will be there to greet you on the other side. When the Christ came to stand in the place of Israel, to be Israel, what would we expect of him but that he would suffer judgement because of sin before being vindicated and glorified on judgement's far side?

Fast forward many hundreds of years and that is precisely what Jesus the Christ does—suffering and dying for sin, and rising triumphant to the place of glory. And in all this, says Peter to his readers, you're better placed than the prophets of old or the angels of heaven—because not only has the promise now been fulfilled, but it has all been clearly revealed to you "through those who preached the good news to you by the Holy Spirit sent from heaven".

What does this mean? The preaching of the good news is clear enough. Some evangelists had come and announced the gospel to them—the news that Jesus Christ had died for sin and risen to glory, and that they should turn back to him and put their faith in him. But the evangelists had done their work "by the Holy Spirit sent from heaven"; the Holy Spirit was in some sense also the evangelist. Just as the Spirit of Christ was at work in the prophets, so the same Spirit was at work in and through the evangelists—which is to say that the Spirit gave them the apostolic message to say and the boldness to say it, and also worked in the hearts of their hearers to elicit a response.

Peter's readers had experienced that response. They had been born again to a living hope (1:3), born again not of perishable seed but imperishable seed, namely the living and abiding word of God, the gospel that was preached to them (1:23-25).

A breathtaking picture emerges from this extraordinary little paragraph in 1 Peter. In fulfilment of his ancient plans, God has brought salvation by sending his Christ to pass through suffering to glory. He is now announcing this momentous news to the world by his Holy Spirit working through human evangelists, and by this method he is saving people, bringing them to new birth, and granting them an eternal, unshakeable, incorruptible inheritance in his eternal kingdom.

What God is doing now

This is what God is now doing in the world: Spirit-backed gospel preaching leading to the salvation of souls. It's his program, his agenda, his priority, his focus, his project, or whatever business-related metaphor you'd like to use. And by it, he is gathering a new Christ-centred people as his very own; a quiet, steadily growing profusion of leaves on the great vine of his kingdom.

This is what we see happening in Acts. We call it the Acts of the Apostles, but a better name would perhaps be 'The Acts of the word and Spirit of God through the Apostles', because that's how it seems to go. The apostolic task is to preach; to bear witness; to proclaim the word; and to do so under the power and enabling of God's Spirit. The apostles affirm this priority in Acts 6 when they indicate how determined they are to keep devoting themselves "to prayer and to the ministry of the word".

Then four times in Acts we are told that the "word of God (or the Lord)" increased and multiplied and spread, almost as if it had a life of its own. And at every step of this growth, the Spirit is there at work, filling the preachers with boldness and the power to speak, and granting faith and new life to those who hear—such as in the massively significant conversion of Cornelius and his house in Acts 10, where the Holy Spirit falls on "all who heard the word", even as Peter is speaking. It is interesting how this event is later described, when Peter relates the story in Jerusalem in chapter 11. When Peter is finished, even those in the sceptical circumcision party are forced to glorify God and say, "Then to the Gentiles also God has granted repentance that leads to life". Salvation and new life come as the word is preached, but only if God grants repentance—only if the Holy Spirit falls on those who hear the word, so that their dead hearts might spring to life in response.

Paul describes the progress of the gospel among the Colossians in much the same way. Epaphras had preached the word of truth to them, and Paul thanks God that when they heard it they responded with faith. And as in Acts, Paul then describes the gospel as having a vibrant, growing life of its own: "...the gospel, which has come to you, as indeed in the whole world it is bearing fruit and growing—as it also does among you, since the day you heard it and understood the grace of God in truth..." (Col 1:5-6).

Throughout the world, the gospel is spreading, propagating,

budding, flowering, bearing fruit. People hear it and by God's mercy respond and are saved. But it doesn't stop there. Once the gospel is planted in someone's life and takes root, it keeps growing in them. Their lives bear fruit. They grow in love and godliness and knowledge and spiritual wisdom, so that they walk in a manner worthy of their calling, fully pleasing to the Father, bearing fruit in every good work (Col 1:9-10, 2:6-7).

We talk a lot these days about church growth. And when we think about our lack of growth, we think of the lack of growth of our particular congregation: the stagnation or decline in numbers, the wobbly state of the finances, and possibly the looming property issues.

But it's interesting how little the New Testament talks about church growth, and how often it talks about 'gospel growth' or the increase of the 'word'. The focus is on the progress of the Spirit-backed word of God as it makes its way in the world, according to God's plan. Returning to our vine metaphor, the vine is the Spirit-empowered word, spreading and growing throughout the world, drawing people out of the kingdom of darkness into the light-filled kingdom of God's beloved Son, and then bearing fruit in their lives as they grow in the knowledge and love of God. The vine is Jesus, and as we are grafted into him, we bear fruit (John 15:1-11).

This results, of course, in individual congregations growing and being built. But the emphasis is not on the growth of the congregation as a structure—in numbers, finances and success—but on the growth of the gospel, as it is spoken and re-spoken under the power of the Spirit. In fact, New Testament congregations, as far as we can tell, were usually small gatherings meeting in houses. They were outwardly unimpressive, and had minimal infrastructure. But God kept drawing people into them by the gospel. Or to put it another way, Christ kept doing what he said he would do in Matthew 16. He kept building his church.

Three implications

Now you may not be in the habit of thinking about God's work in the world in precisely these terms, but I trust you see the implications. There are several, and we will tease them out in the coming chapters. But at this point, we should note three important consequences of this view of God's purposes in the world.

The first and most obvious is that if this is really what God is doing in our world then it is time to say goodbye to our small and self-oriented ambitions, and to abandon ourselves to the cause of Christ and his gospel. God has a plan that will determine the destiny of every person and nation in the world, and it is unfolding here and now as the gospel of Christ is preached and the Holy Spirit is poured out. Is there anything more vital to be doing in our world? It is more important than our jobs, our families, our pastimes—yes, even more important than the comfort and security of familiar church life. We need to recapture the radicalism of what Jesus said to the young man who wanted to return and bury his father: "Leave the dead to bury their own dead. But as for you, go and proclaim the kingdom of God" (Luke 9:60).

The second implication is that the growth God is looking for in our world is growth in *people*. He is working through his word and Spirit to draw people into his kingdom, to see them born again as new creations, and to see them mature and bear fruit as servants of Christ. Whatever other signs of life and growth we might look for in our congregations—involvement, activities, newcomers, finances, number of staff, buildings, and so on—the only growth that has any significance in God's plans is the growth of believers. This is what the growing vine really is: it is individual, born-again believers, grafted into Christ by his word and Spirit, and drawn into mutually edifying fellowship with one another.

The third momentous implication is that this people-growth happens only through the power of God's Spirit as he applies his word to people's hearts. That's the way people are converted, and that's the way people grow in maturity in Christ. We plant and water, but God gives the growth. We speak God's word to someone, and the Spirit enables a response. This can happen individually, in small groups, and in large groups. It can happen over the back fence, over dinner, or over morning tea at church. It can happen in a pulpit or on a patio. It can be the formal exposition or study of a Bible passage, or someone speaking some Scripture-based truth without even referring to the Bible.

However, despite the almost limitless number of contexts in which it might happen, what happens is the same: a Christian brings a truth from God's word to someone else, praying that God would make that word bear fruit through the inward working of his Spirit.

That's vine work. Everything else is trellis.

Chapter 4

Is every Christian a vine-worker?

In the previous chapter we put forward a simple but profound proposition: that the work God is doing in the world now, in these last days between the first and second comings of Christ, is to gather people into his kingdom through the prayerful proclamation of the gospel. God is growing his vine through his word and Spirit.

Most evangelical Christians would no doubt agree with these ideas. Yes, they would say: Christian growth certainly does happen because God does it through his word under the life-giving power of his Spirit. And yes, they would agree: this means that the two fundamental activities of Christian ministry are *proclaiming* (speaking the word) and *praying* (calling upon God to pour out his Spirit to make the word effective in people's hearts).

Where it all gets trickier is in translating these motherhood statements into action in our churches. In particular, how are we to think about the ministry of all Christians as opposed to the ministry of designated pastors, teachers and evangelists? What is the ministry of the many, and how does it relate to the ministry of the few?

Or to put it more sharply, *who really does the vine work?* Is it mainly the job of the pastor-teachers and evangelists to tend and propagate the vine through their ministry of the word? Is

the main contribution of the rest of the congregation to support
and aid that work by maintaining and strengthening the trellis?
Or do all Christians play a part in vine work?

These are not simple questions, and they have been
answered in different ways in the history of Christianity. Even
since the Reformation, with its insistence on the priesthood of
all believers, Christians have adopted different models and
traditions of ministry—some in which the leader or pastor is so
central and dominant that the congregation are little more than
spectators, and others in which anti-clericalism has gone so far
as to abolish the role of 'pastor' or 'overseer' altogether.

What does the Bible say?

Disciples confessing

At the most basic level, the Bible says that Jesus doesn't have two
classes of disciple: those who abandon their lives to his service
and those who don't. The call to discipleship is the same for all.
Jesus says, "If anyone would come after me, let him deny himself
and take up his cross and follow me. For whoever would save his
life will lose it, but whoever loses his life for my sake and the
gospel's will save it" (Mark 8:34-35). There are not two sorts of
disciples—the inner core who really serve Jesus and his gospel,
and the rest. To be a disciple is to be a slave of Christ and to
confess his name openly before others: "So everyone who
acknowledges me before men, I also will acknowledge before my
Father who is in heaven, but whoever denies me before men, I
also will deny before my Father who is in heaven" (Matt 10:32-33).

The call to discipleship is thus a call to confess our
allegiance to Jesus in the face of a hostile world; to serve him
and his mission, whatever the cost. Don't bother attending your
dad's funeral, Jesus says to a passing enquiry: "Leave the dead
to bury their own dead. But as for you, go and proclaim the
kingdom of God" (Luke 9:60).

The Great Commission, in other words, is not just for the Eleven. It's the basic agenda for all disciples. To be a disciple is to be a disciple-maker.

The radicalism of this demand often feels a world away from the ordinariness of our normal Christian habits and customs. We go to church, where we sing a few songs, try to concentrate on the prayers, and hear a sermon. We chat to people afterwards, and then go home for a normal week of work or study or whatever it is that we do, in time to come again next week. We might read our Bible and pray during the week. We may even attend a small group. But would someone observing from outside say: "Look: there is someone who has abandoned his life to Jesus Christ and his mission"?

When we look at the early disciples in the book of Acts, we see this confession and allegiance being worked out in practice, in the face of opposition and persecution. There is no doubt that the apostles played a leading role in testifying to Jesus, and in teaching and preaching, but they weren't the only ones making their confession publicly. As the magnificent prayer for boldness in Acts 4 makes clear, the early Christian disciples all regarded themselves as "servants" of Jesus, and all were given the Holy Spirit to speak out in his name:

> "And now, Lord, look upon their threats and grant to your servants to continue to speak your word with all boldness, while you stretch out your hand to heal, and signs and wonders are performed through the name of your holy servant Jesus." And when they had prayed, the place in which they were gathered together was shaken, and they were all filled with the Holy Spirit and continued to speak the word of God with boldness. (Acts 4:29-31)

That all the disciples were speaking boldly in the name of Jesus shouldn't surprise us in Acts 4, because Acts 2 tells us to expect it. When the Holy Spirit descends so strikingly on the assembled disciples, he descends upon them all, and they all start declaring "the mighty works of God", as verse 11 puts it.

This, says Peter, is only what the prophet Joel said would happen. In the "last days", says Joel, when God's Spirit was poured out on all flesh, everyone would prophesy—the young, the old, men and women, all the way down to the servants of the household—all would declare the word of the Lord (Acts 2:16-18). All would testify to Jesus, because the "testimony of Jesus is the spirit of prophecy" (Rev 19:10).

This pattern continues throughout the New Testament. There are of course leaders, teachers, elders, overseers, pastors and evangelists—people who have leading roles and responsibilities in declaring God's word and shepherding his people—but alongside these, there is a constant stream of references to the 'word ministry' of each and every Christian. Speaking God's word for the growth of the vine is the work not of the few but of the many. Let's look at a few examples.

Speaking the word to one another

In Ephesians 4, Paul famously lists the gifts that the ascended Christ has given the church—apostles, prophets, evangelists and pastor-teachers. And, just as famously, he says that the work of these foundational word ministries is to "equip the saints for the work of ministry" (ESV) or to "prepare God's people for works of service" (NIV). Older translations put a very significant comma between "equip the saints" and "for the work of ministry", taking the verse to mean that the job of the foundational word ministers was the equipping of the saints *and* the work of ministry. Their ministry included equipping the saints—not that they were to equip the saints for the ministry that the saints themselves would exercise.

There are good reasons to think that the older translations are actually closer to the mark. However, when we look at the verses that follow, we see that it doesn't make an enormous difference to our investigation. Paul goes on to say that the goal of all this ministry (whoever is doing it) is the building of the body of Christ to unified, doctrinally sound maturity. We are not to be tossed here and there by every wind of doctrine: "Rather, speaking the truth in love, we are to grow up in every way into him who is the head, into Christ, from whom the whole body, joined and held together by every joint with which it is equipped, when each part is working properly, makes the body grow so that it builds itself up in love" (Eph 4:15-16).

The picture here is of all the different parts of the body fulfilling their proper function, each part working with the others for the growth of the body. But what is common across this multifarious function of different body parts is "speaking the truth in love". We may each do this in different ways, in different contexts and with different levels of effectiveness, but the basic methodology of body growth is that all the members "speak the truth in love", one to another.

We see a similar picture as we read on into chapter 5 of Ephesians. When Paul exhorts them to "be filled with the Spirit" rather than with wine, the result will be that they speak to one another "in psalms and hymns and spiritual songs", as opposed to the kind of speech and singing that tends to follow from too much wine. The work of the indwelling Spirit will lead the Ephesians in spiritual speech to one another, in this case via singing.

But it's not only by singing. A few verses later, in Ephesians 6:4, fathers are urged to raise their children in the instruction of the Lord. Teaching within the family is a vital word ministry exercised by all fathers (and mothers). The requirements for elders (in 1 Timothy 3 and Titus 1) assume that godly heads of households would be teaching their families the word of God.

A related point comes out in Colossians 3: "Let the word of Christ dwell in you richly, teaching and admonishing one another in all wisdom, singing psalms and hymns and spiritual songs, with thankfulness in your hearts to God" (Col 3:16). This time it's the word of Christ that is dwelling in their midst, rather than the Spirit, but the result is the same—which shouldn't surprise us! What ensues is godly encouraging speech to one another, in this case teaching and admonishing. Whether the singing is how the teaching and admonishing takes place, or another result of having the word dwell richly, is hard to say grammatically. It makes very little difference. The point is that all the Colossians are to teach and admonish one another.

Romans 15:14 also assumes that Christians will be teaching and instructing one another: "I myself am satisfied about you, my brothers, that you yourselves are full of goodness, filled with all knowledge and able to instruct one another".

The writer to the Hebrews twice makes the same point. Firstly, in chapter 3, he says:

> Take care, brothers, lest there be in any of you an evil,
> unbelieving heart, leading you to fall away from the
> living God. But exhort one another every day, as long as
> it is called 'today', that none of you may be hardened by
> the deceitfulness of sin. (Heb 3:12-13)

This can only mean that God wants all Christians to be speaking to each other regularly, urging and encouraging each other to stick with Christ. He makes a very similar point in chapter 10, in one of the few verses in the entire New Testament that tell Christians to 'go to church':

> And let us consider how to stir up one another to love and
> good works, not neglecting to meet together, as is the
> habit of some, but encouraging one another, and all the
> more as you see the Day drawing near. (Heb 10:24-25)

A central purpose of getting together, says the writer, is mutual encouragement; to spur one another on to love and good works as we wait for the day of Christ. How this can happen without us opening our mouths and speaking to each other is hard to understand.

But of all the parts of the New Testament that deal with the ministry of the few and of the many, the clearest and most helpful is Paul's first letter to the arrogant, gifted, divided, sin-prone Corinthians.

Now the Corinthians had real problems, both over the nature of leadership and over how each member could contribute to the edification of the congregation. In both cases, they seemed to think too highly—too highly of different leaders, so that factions emerged in the congregation depending on which leader you followed; and too highly of themselves and their gifts, so that their gatherings became a chaotic exercise in one-upmanship, with everyone more focused on 'using their gifts' than on actually encouraging other people.

Paul deals with the leadership question in 1 Corinthians 1-4. His basic message is that the gospel of Christ crucified gives the model for Christian leadership in ministry. It's a ministry exercised in apparent weakness and foolishness, and yet by God's Spirit it brings salvation. Paul and Apollos are just manual labourers in God's field. It's God who gives the growth, and so any factionalism around the qualities of different leaders is absurd.

In chapters 11-14, Paul turns to the conduct of their congregational gatherings and the contribution each member is to make. There is, of course, a long history of debate about many of the details of these chapters (to do with the nature of miraculous gifts and speaking in tongues, not to mention the regulations for head covering in chapter 11 and the place of women in ministry). However, in relation to our investigation about the 'ministry of the many' the important points are clear, and could be summarized as follows:

- Chapter 11 envisages that both men and women will pray and prophesy as a matter of course in the gathering.[1]

- Chapter 12 emphasizes that while there is a variety of gifts and ministries, we are all members of the one body in Christ Jesus.
- Chapter 13 gives the single criterion for the exercise of these gifts: love. We each make our contribution not for our own good, but for the good of others.

This means (as chapter 14 goes on to say) that we should seek and exercise those gifts that do most good to others, those gifts that build (or 'edify') the congregation. Prophecy gets top marks (over tongues, for example), because it consists of intelligible, edifying words.

The summary verse is 14:26:

> What then, brothers? When you come together, each
> one has a hymn, a lesson, a revelation, a tongue, or an
> interpretation. Let all things be done for building up.

These chapters repay some careful reading because they beautifully capture both the singularity and the diversity of the ministry of each congregation member. We are not all the same. Not everyone is a 'teacher' or a 'prophet', and the way we bring encouragement and edification to the gathering will vary according to God's gifting. But everyone should be pursuing the same goal, which is to edify the congregation in love; and this edification takes place through speech (intelligible speech, that is), whether a word of exhortation, a hymn, a revelation, a tongue-with-interpretation, or a prophecy.

We may all build (edify) in different ways, but we are all builders. We do not all have the same function, but we are all urged to abound in "the work of the Lord, knowing that in the Lord your labour is not in vain" (1 Cor 15:58). Interestingly, Paul uses exactly the same phrase just a few verses later to describe his own ministry and Timothy's: "When Timothy comes, see that you put him at ease among you, for he is doing *the work of the Lord*, as I am" (1 Cor 16:10).

Simply by virtue of being a disciple of Jesus and filled with the Holy Spirit of the new covenant, all Christians have the privilege, joy and responsibility of being involved in the work God is doing in our world, the "work of the Lord". And the fundamental way we do this is by speaking the truth of God to other people in dependence on the Holy Spirit.

Is every Christian a missionary?

Most of the references we've looked at in the epistles refer to Christians speaking the truth of God's word to one another. But what of speaking the word to non-Christians?

It is somewhat surprising that the New Testament contains relatively few exhortations for ordinary believers to speak the gospel to others. Scholars and missiologists have debated the reasons for this. One possible answer lies in the reality that the gospel was advancing irresistibly from one region to another, powerfully breaking into first-century society, saving individuals and forming communities of Christ. The first believers were inevitably caught up in this dynamic, Spirit-inspired movement and could not have avoided 'evangelism', even if they had wanted to. If you stuck your head up as a convert to Christ, whether Jew, God-fearing Gentile or pagan, you were in danger of getting it lopped off. At the very least, you would be asked to give a reason for your new hope (cf. 1 Pet 3:13-16).

The new disciples at Thessalonica were a case in point. The gospel had come to them not simply with human words, but powerfully and with deep conviction (1 Thess 1:5). They had become imitators of Paul and of the Lord Jesus in the sense that they welcomed the message of truth with Spirit-inspired joy, despite persecution. And not surprisingly these young converts became missionaries without even joining a mission agency.

And you became imitators of us and of the Lord, for you received the word in much affliction, with the joy of the Holy Spirit, so that you became an example to all the believers in Macedonia and in Achaia. For not only has the word of the Lord sounded forth from you in Macedonia and Achaia, but your faith in God has gone forth everywhere, so that we need not say anything. For they themselves report concerning us the kind of reception we had among you, and how you turned to God from idols to serve the living and true God, and to wait for his Son from heaven, whom he raised from the dead, Jesus who delivers us from the wrath to come. (1 Thess 1:6-10)

The gospel had so transformed their world view, and the Holy Spirit had so enlivened them, that the word of the Lord "sounded forth" from the Thessalonians, both locally and further afield. The Greek word used here (*execheō*) conveys the picture of God's word ringing out from them as the sound from a clanging bell. They could not keep the message to themselves, even though their social relationships were now very difficult. Wherever Paul went, he heard this report of how the Thessalonians had welcomed the gospel and turned to the living and true God.

Some commentators cannot envisage that these new Christians would have engaged in missionary activity, and so claim that it was the report of their conversion that was spread abroad. But this is not what the text says—it was the word of the Lord itself that rang out from them. Anyway, it is a false distinction. How could the report have rung out without the content of the gospel also being communicated?

My point is that it was inevitable and natural that these new converts, whose religious and social life had been turned upside down, would have spoken to others about the gospel that had transformed them. They would not have had to be *told* to evangelize. How could they have avoided explaining what had happened to them, whether at the meat market or a dinner party?

Which brings us to a central passage on this issue:

> So, whether you eat or drink, or whatever you do, do all
> to the glory of God. Give no offense to Jews or to Greeks
> or to the church of God, just as I try to please everyone
> in everything I do, not seeking my own advantage, but
> that of many, that they may be saved.
>
> Be imitators of me, as I am of Christ. (1 Cor 10:31-11:1)

Becoming a Christian in first-century Corinth raised the social dilemma of which dinner parties to attend, and what to eat when you got there. Unlike our modern Western societies (but like other cultures in the world today), dining and religious practice were integrally related. So what should new Christians do about eating "food offered to idols" (1 Cor 8:1)? The 'weaker' brother thinks this is sinful (8:7-8). Paul knows he is free to eat idol meat because there is only one God and one Lord, but he does not exercise his freedom so as to avoid being a stumbling block to others (8:4-13).

The exercise of our Christian freedom is the big theme of these chapters. Paul knows he is "free from all", but he intentionally makes himself a slave to everyone—whether to Jews, Gentiles or 'weak' Christians (1 Cor 9:19-23). And why does he curtail his freedom and forfeit his rights? His goal is to "win more of them" (v. 19), to "save some" (v. 22), "for the sake of the gospel" (v. 23). The goal of his social flexibility was the salvation of others.

It is very striking that Paul calls upon ordinary believers in Corinth to be imitators of him, as he is of Christ. And this imitating is not in some general sense, but in *actively seeking the salvation of others*. They are not to seek their own advantage "but that of many, that they may be saved" (10:33). In decisions about food and drink, and in all matters, the goal is the glory of God (v. 31). They must not cause anyone to stumble in faith, whether Jew, Gentile or a (weak) brother in the church of God (v. 32). Although the mission responsibilities and activities of the Corinthians would have differed from Paul's, their orientation in life was to be the same. Their whole aim was to be the glory of God in the salvation of others.

The Christian without a missionary heart is an anomaly. The missionary heart will be seen in all kinds of ways: in prayers for the lost, in making sure our behaviour offends no-one, in gospel conversations with friends (at dinner parties!), and in making every effort to save some. We are slaves without rights, even though we are free (cf. 2 Cor 4:5; Phil 2:7).

There are other important passages that portray the missionary heart and activity of ordinary disciples.

Disciples are called to a distinctive, 'salty' lifestyle characterized by good deeds and righteousness. By living this way we shine as lights in the world, attracting praise not to ourselves but to God our Father (Matt 5:13-16). We are called to pray for the bold proclamation of the gospel in the world (Col 4:2-3). Our conversation with outsiders should be gracious yet provocative, giving appropriate answers to the questions that are prompted by our way of life (Col 4:5-6). The sound doctrine of the gospel produces a radical Christian way of life that gives no grounds for slander, and makes the teaching of the gospel attractive to the world (Titus 2:1-10). Like God's chosen people Israel, Christians both corporately and privately are to make God known to the nations by declaring his mercies in the gospel and by living a holy life (1 Pet 2:9-12, 3:1-2). Even in the midst of persecution, believers are to surrender to the lordship of Christ and gently give a defence of the hope we have in the gospel (1 Pet 3:15).

We have to conclude that a Christian with no passion for

the lost is in serious need of self-examination and repentance. Even the atheists have worked this out. Penn Jillette is an avowed and vocal atheist, and one-half of the famous comic-illusionist act Penn and Teller. He was evangelized by a polite and impressive man, and had this to say about the experience:

> "...I've always said, you know, that I don't respect people who don't proselytize. I don't respect that at all. If you believe that there's a heaven and hell, and people could be going to hell, or not getting eternal life or whatever, and you think that, well, it's not really worth telling them this because it would make it socially awkward... How much do you have to hate somebody to not proselytize? How much do you have to hate somebody to believe that everlasting life is possible and not tell them that? I mean, if I believed beyond a shadow of a doubt that a truck was coming at you, and you didn't believe it, and that truck was bearing down on you, there is a certain point where I tackle you. And this is more important than that..."[2]

Whenever and however to whomever

The New Testament envisages that all Christian disciples will be prayerful speakers of God's word, in a multitude of different ways and contexts.

In each context, the message is essentially the same. It's not as if we come to know Christ through the gospel word but then use a fundamentally different message to encourage each other as Christians. The 'word of God', the message that he has revealed in and through Christ by his Spirit—this is what converts us, and it is also what causes us to grow, bearing the fruit of godliness. The vine grows, both in the number of leaves and in their quality and maturity, through the word and Spirit—

through God's truth being heard, and the Spirit making it effective in people's hearts.

This happens in our gatherings, but it also happens day by day as Christians speak the truth to each other and exhort one another to stay strong (Eph 4:25; Heb 3:13). It happens in the home as fathers bring up their children in the discipline and instruction of the Lord (Eph 6:4). It happens in the world as we proclaim the excellencies of Christ before the nations (1 Pet 2:9), or engage in gracious, salty conversations with outsiders (Col 4:5-6), or give gentle, respectful answers about the Christian hope (1 Pet 3:15-16).

Let's pause for a moment, and tease out what this means in practice. Here, off the top of my head, are ten ways in which any Christian might "speak the truth in love" to someone else in the name of Christ, and thus participate in God's great work in the world:

- Geoff is asked by his workmate Peter what he did on the weekend, and he replies that he heard an excellent sermon in church that helped him understand for the first time what was really wrong with the world. When Peter asks him to elaborate, Geoff explains why sin and God's judgement explain the problems in our world. Geoff continues to pray for Peter that these sorts of opportunities would continue and that Peter's heart would be softened to respond to the message.
- Sarah's teenage son is having real problems at high school, and as they talk about it at night, she reassures him that God is stronger and more faithful than any friend, and prays with him.
- Bill is chatting to George after church, and shares with him how encouraged he was by a particular verse in the Bible that day.
- Michael meets one to one every fortnight over breakfast

with his mate Steve, who is a newish Christian. They use the *Just for Starters* set of Bible studies to work through some of the basic issues of living the Christian life.

- Alison is worried about her friend Debbie, who struggles with anxiety and has been missing church quite a lot. Alison writes her a one-page letter, offering encouragement, quoting a few Bible verses, and offering to get together to pray.

- Warren goes to a Bible study group each week at Jim's house with six other people. He makes sure that he has read and thought about the passage before he goes, and prays that God would help him to say true and encouraging things in the group.

- Irene is quite elderly and finds it hard to get out, but she phones her friend Jean every second day, talks to her about the Bible passage she has read that morning and prays with her over the phone.

- Clare has been praying for her friend Shirley for months, and finally invites her to an evangelistic evening that her church is running. On the way home in the car, Clare talks to Shirley about the message, and does her best to answer Shirley's questions.

- Trevor rearranges his work schedule so that he can take Wednesday morning off to teach Scripture classes in his local primary school. He and his wife end up doing this for many years, and have an enormous impact on the lives of kids and teachers at their local school.

- At Phil's church, they take a few minutes during the Sunday meeting for a congregation member to give a testimony or to bring an encouraging word to the congregation. This Sunday it's Phil's turn, and he tells how the teaching of Ephesians 5 has turned his marriage around.

The names and details have been changed slightly, but these are real examples of Christians prayerfully bringing the truth of

God to other people. It can happen at home, at work, over the back fence, at church, in small groups, in a coffee shop—anywhere. But that it happens is vital, because this is the "work of the Lord"; this is the Great Commission in action; this is the vine work that all Christians can and should be engaged in.

For those who like to think more systematically, here's another way of looking at the different ways Christians can be involved in prayerfully bringing the word of God to others. We all exist in three spheres or contexts of life: our family or home life; our interaction with friends, colleagues, neighbours and the wider community; and fellowship with God's people in our congregations. How might we speak the truth of God's word in each of these contexts?

	Home	Congregation	Community
One to one	• Bible reading and prayer with children • Bible reading and prayer with spouse • Writing letters to extended family • Bringing the Bible to bear in daily conversations	• Following up a new Christian (basic Bible studies etc.) • Bible reading and prayer one to one with someone • The 'ministry of the pew'[3] • Following up newcomers and visitors to church	• Inviting people to evangelistic events • Giving away books, tracts and sermons • Giving your personal testimony • Walk-up evangelism • Friendship evangelism • Water-cooler conversations (answering common questions)
Small groups	• Family Bible reading and prayer	• Meeting with small group for prayer and Bible study • Teaching Sunday school or youth group • Men's and women's groups	• Small-group based evangelism (courses etc.) • Teaching Scripture or Bible classes in schools
Large groups	• Inserting Christian content at birthdays and family gatherings (e.g. sharing a Bible verse and praying)	• Occasional preaching • Giving a testimony and/or encouragement • Leading singing • Reading the Bible	• Giving an evangelistic talk or testimony (e.g. at a men's breakfast)

If you want yet another way of expressing the same point, what we are really talking about is a *Bible-reading movement*—in families, in churches, in neighbourhoods, in workplaces, everywhere. Imagine if all Christians, as a normal part of their discipleship, were caught up in a web of regular Bible reading—not only digging into the word privately, but reading it with their children before bed, with their spouse over breakfast, with a non-Christian colleague at work once a week over lunch, with a new Christian for follow-up once a fortnight for mutual encouragement, and with a mature Christian friend once a month for mutual encouragement.

It would be a chaotic web of personal relationships, prayer and Bible reading—more of a movement than a program—but at another level it would be profoundly simple and within reach of all.

It's an exciting thought! And it is hardly a controversial or outrageous idea. Most pastors would love their congregation to be involved in this kind of everyday Bible ministry. Who could argue against it?

However, if we pause to reflect on the implications of this vision of vine work by every Christian, many of our most cherished assumptions about church, ministry, evangelism and congregational life are called into question.

For a start, it radically dissolves many of the traditional distinctions between 'clergy' and 'laity'. Many of us minister in contexts where the unspoken (or even spoken!) assumption is that it is the pastor's job to build the church, and the members' job to receive that ministry and to support it through involvement in a range of jobs and roles—counting the money, organizing morning tea, ushering, serving on committees, and so on. The pastor (or pastoral staff team) is really the one who does the vine work and the rest of us do what we can to maintain the trellis, not least by giving money.

The New Testament's vision of ministry is quite different. The pastors and elders certainly take the lead in vine work (in prayer and proclamation), and are responsible for guarding and teaching the word and maintaining the gold standard of sound doctrine. But one of the effects of this work is to equip and release the members to do vine work themselves. We saw this in Ephesians where the whole congregation was to "speak the truth in love" as a result of the ministry of the pastor-teachers. We also catch an interesting glimpse of it in Paul's letter to Titus, where the elders must "hold firm to the trustworthy word as taught, so that [they] may be able to give instruction in sound doctrine and also to rebuke those who contradict it" (Titus 1:9). One of the effects of teaching this sound doctrine is that the congregation will know how to encourage and train each other—such as the older women in chapter 2, who are to "teach what is good, and so train the young women to love their husbands and children" (2:3-4).

In other words, we are all engaged in "the work of the Lord" (1 Cor 15:58). We all do our part in helping the vine to grow through prayerfully speaking the word, whenever and however we can. Luther put it with typical sharpness like this:

> The ministry of the Word belongs to all. To bind and to loose clearly is nothing else than to proclaim and to apply the gospel. For what is it to loose, if not to announce the forgiveness of sins before God? What is it to bind, except to withdraw the gospel and to declare the retention of sins? Whether they [that is, the Roman Catholic Church] want to or not, they must concede that the keys are the exercise of the ministry of the Word and belong to all Christians.[4]

Does this sound too extreme? Or too demanding on the struggling Christians you know? Or just too hard to persuade people of?

We need to think further about the nature of the normal Christian life.

Endnotes

1. We are not able to go into detail at this point about the (often controversial) question of the ministries of men and women within congregations. However, just as the New Testament envisages the involvement and 'word ministry' of all Christians while preserving a unique leadership role for pastors, teachers and elders, so it also envisages some form of word ministry for women in the congregation (e.g. 1 Cor 11:4-5) while preserving a unique teaching and leadership role for men (cf. 1 Cor 14:33-35; 1 Tim 2:11-12).
2. www.youtube.com/watch?v=fa9JE_ZVL88
3. The 'ministry of the pew' refers to the ministry every Christian can have each Sunday in church. For more details see Col Marshall, 'The ministry of the pew', *The Briefing*, vol. 131, 21 March 1994: www.matthiasmedia.com.au/briefing/library/1855/
4. Martin Luther, 'Concerning the Ministry', in *Luther's Works*, vol. 40, *Church and Ministry II*, ed. Conrad Bergendoff and Helmut T Lehmann, Muhlenberg Press, Philadelphia, 1958, p. 27. The mention of 'keys' and, indeed, the entire quote is in reference to Matthew 16:19: "I will give you the keys of the kingdom of heaven, and whatever you bind on earth shall be bound in heaven, and whatever you loose on earth shall be loosed in heaven".

Chapter 5

Guilt or grace?

e've been arguing that all Christians are vine-workers; that all are engaged in "the work of the Lord". In the chapters that follow, we'll be exploring how pastors and leaders play a crucial role in training and encouraging their people as fellow labourers in this work. However, before we get there, it's worth pausing to discuss a common set of objections.

Is it really true, we often get asked, that the normal Christian life includes disciple-making? What about those who are barely hanging on to faith in Christ? Should we make them feel bad because they aren't out there sharing the gospel or encouraging someone else in the faith or being 'trained in ministry'? Aren't we just making the average struggling Christian feel guilty? Or worse, aren't we in danger of creating a new kind of legalism, where being 'involved in disciple-making' becomes the standard you have to meet to win the approval of your pastor (if not of God)? Do we end up creating two classes of Christians: the 'keenies' and the rest?

These are legitimate and important questions, and at their heart is a question about the normal Christian life. There is no better place to answer this than from Paul's extraordinary letter from prison to the Philippians.

Partners in the gospel of grace

Paul wrote his letter to the Christians at Philippi while enjoying the 'hospitality' of the Roman authorities. For daring to preach Christ as the true king rather than Caesar, Paul was in prison, probably in Rome, and facing the very real prospect of execution (1:13-14, 21).

How would you react if your pastor was imprisoned for preaching Christ as the only true God? Perhaps you would disown him because of embarrassment, shame or the fear of what you might lose. If someone challenged you, you might say: "Oh, I don't really know him very well. I've only actually been to his church a few times. I always thought he was a bit extreme."

Then again, maybe you would find the strength to stand in solidarity with him—by sending gifts, praying, accepting the persecution of the authorities, and defiantly continuing to preach the same message of Christ. Perhaps you would say: "Yes, my pastor is in prison for preaching Christ. And they can come and lock me up too if they want to, because I will not stop confessing the truth—that Jesus Christ is the risen Lord of all."

What would you do?

Paul's letter opens with a prayer of great joy because the Philippians have remained in solidarity with him in the gospel "from the first day until now". The Philippians didn't disown or abandon their imprisoned apostle; they stood with him. And the word that Paul keeps using throughout the letter to describe this solidarity is 'partnership'. In Greek, it is *koinōnia*, the word we often translate as 'fellowship'.

The fellowship that the Philippians shared with Paul was not a cup of tea after church, or a pleasant evening of Bible study. The Philippians and Paul were sharers together in *God's grace* through Jesus Christ (1:7). Like Paul, the Philippians were looking forward to the day of Christ, when by his death and resurrection they would be counted pure and blameless and filled with the fruit of righteousness (1:9-11, 3:8-10). God himself had begun a good work in them, and would bring it to completion (1:6).

The partnership they shared in the gospel was not a way of securing their right standing before God. If anyone might have had a reason to boast before God and declare himself righteous, it would have been Paul himself—that "Hebrew of Hebrews" (3:5). But the gospel he preached rendered all human striving for righteousness pathetic and pointless:

> But whatever gain I had, I counted as loss for the sake of Christ. Indeed, I count everything as loss because of the surpassing worth of knowing Christ Jesus my Lord. For his sake I have suffered the loss of all things and count them as rubbish, in order that I may gain Christ and be found in him, not having a righteousness of my own that comes from the law, but that which comes through faith in Christ, the righteousness from God that depends on faith... (Phil 3:7-9)

This is the gospel the Philippians had heard and, by God's grace, believed. It was a gospel about a suffering Christ who died and rose to bring righteousness and salvation to his people. Embracing this gospel meant being willing to suffer like Christ himself. In fact, Paul puts it even more strongly than that. He says that standing up for the gospel, and being called to suffer for Christ, is itself a gift of God's grace:

> It is right for me to feel this way about you all, because I hold you in my heart, for you are all partakers with me of grace, both in my imprisonment and in the defence and confirmation of the gospel. (Phil 1:7)

> For it has been granted to you that for the sake of Christ you should not only believe in him but also suffer for his sake... (Phil 1:29)

And so Paul urges the ordinary everyday Christians in Philippi to remain strong in their gospel partnership; to keep standing up for Christ in the face of hostility and persecution. To live this way, he says, is merely to live in a manner worthy of the gospel itself:

> Only let your manner of life be worthy of the gospel of Christ, so that whether I come and see you or am absent, I may hear of you that you are standing firm in one spirit, with one mind striving side by side for the faith of the gospel, and not frightened in anything by your opponents. This is a clear sign to them of their destruction, but of your salvation, and that from God. For it has been granted to you that for the sake of Christ you should not only believe in him but also suffer for his sake, engaged in the same conflict that you saw I had and now hear that I still have. (Phil 1:27-30)

The Greek word behind "let your manner of life" in verse 27 means to "live as a citizen". The noun form of the word is used in 3:20: "But our *citizenship* is in heaven, and from it we await a Saviour, the Lord Jesus Christ..."

The Philippians knew very well that they were a Roman colony, with all the privileges and rights of being full citizens of the Empire. But, Paul reminds them, your king is not Caesar, and Rome is not your citizenship; your king is Jesus Christ, and heaven is your citizenship. Live, therefore, in a manner worthy of *that* citizenship. Stand side by side as a united army fighting for *that* king, to his honour and glory.

The ordinary believers in Philippi were not second-class citizens, or support crew hovering behind the front lines. They were to lock arms and strive together "for the faith of the gospel", being neither surprised by the conflict and struggle that would ensue, nor frightened of their opponents. And in doing so, they were engaged in *the same conflict and struggle* that Paul himself had experienced and was still experiencing. They were partners in suffering; partners in the "defence and confirmation of the gospel" (1:7); partners with Paul and with each other.

This is why unity is so important in the congregation, and why complaining, grumbling and discord is so totally out of place. The wonderful passage about the other-person-centred humility of Christ in chapter 2 is, in context, a call for the Philippians to put aside selfish motives and petty rivalries so that they can strive together for the sake of the gospel, shining like beacons in the corrupt society around them:

> Do all things without grumbling or questioning, that
> you may be blameless and innocent, children of God
> without blemish in the midst of a crooked and twisted
> generation, among whom you shine as lights in the
> world, holding fast to the word of life, so that in the day
> of Christ I may be proud that I did not run in vain or
> labour in vain. (Phil 2:14-16)

Scholars have debated whether it should be 'holding fast' in verse 16, or 'holding out'—the implication being that 'holding out' implies an outward-looking evangelistic emphasis, whereas 'holding fast' is more about their own perseverance in the faith. It's hard to imagine the Philippians having any patience with this distinction. For them, 'holding fast' to the gospel as partners with Paul inevitably meant joining with him in striving for the gospel, and accepting the suffering that always followed. It meant standing alongside their imprisoned apostle, and speaking out for the "defence and confirmation of the gospel".

Paul mentions Timothy and Epaphroditus as two out-standing examples for the Philippians to emulate. Timothy is unparalleled in his concern for others rather than himself (2:20-21). He puts the interests of Jesus Christ first, and serves alongside Paul like a son in the family business. Epaphroditus is a Philippian, whom Paul calls "my brother and fellow worker and fellow soldier, and your messenger and minister to my need, for he has been longing for you all and has been distressed because you heard that he was ill" (2:25-26).

Did you get that? Epaphroditus was distressed not because he was ill, but because they heard he was ill. How many of us can say that about our attitude when we are sick?!

Normal Christian partnership

According to Paul, gospel partnership is the normal Christian life. It means standing together united in the gospel, determined to live as citizens of heaven in the midst of our corrupt generation, longing and striving to see the gospel be defended and proclaimed, and bravely copping the conflict, struggle and persecution that inevitably follow.

The practical outworking of this partnership is broad ranging. We see the Philippians praying for Paul (1:19); we see them sharing in his troubles by sending him financial help (4:14-19); we see Philippians like Epaphroditus, Euodia, Syntyche and Clement among Paul's band of co-workers; and we see the Philippians being called to imitate Paul in contending for the gospel despite hostility from without and opposition from within (3:17-4:1).

The gospel itself demands that we stand with our leaders and preachers in profound unity, teamwork and solidarity—not because of their personalities or gifts, but because of our common partnership in the gospel of Jesus Christ. There aren't two classes of Christians—the partners and the spectators. We're all in it together.

One church we have been involved in tried to express this by not having 'membership' of the congregation, but 'partnership'. In our society, when you join as a 'member' of something, it can have connotations of passivity and consumerism. I join a club, and expect certain benefits. The 'partnership' language, on the other hand, communicates immediately that we are signing up for active involvement—for being partners together in a great enterprise: the gospel mission of Christ.

In first-century Philippi, there was no doubt what this involved—a willingness to publicly bind yourself to a new and distrusted 'sect' whose leaders were being thrown in gaol; a determination to stand together with your brothers, come what may, and contend for the gospel; and a self-forgetting commitment to your brothers and sisters in Christ.

None of this was a program of good works to get you into heaven! In fact, legalizers who wanted to put confidence in the flesh were the enemy. But the immeasurable free grace of God that came to them through faith in Christ was not a licence for an easy, comfortable life with a dash of spirituality on the side; rather, it was a passport to a new citizenship of suffering and contending side by side for the gospel.

Paul was their leader, example and fellow soldier in this fight. And this is the pattern we see elsewhere in the New Testament as well. Leaders, pastors and elders are responsible to teach, to warn, to rebuke, and to encourage. They are foremen and organizers, guardians and mobilizers, teachers and models. They provide the conditions under which the rest of the gospel partners can also get on with vine work—with prayerfully speaking God's truth to others.

However, at a profound level, all pastors and elders are also just partners. They do not have a different essence or status, or a fundamentally different task—as if they are the real 'players', and the rest of the congregation are spectators or support crew. A pastor or elder is a vine-worker who has been given a particular responsibility to care for and equip the people for their partnership in the gospel.

Which brings us inevitably to 'training'.

Chapter 6

The heart of training

R eaders of this book may well fall into two categories.
There are some for whom 'training' is something of
a ministry buzzword. They assume they know what it
means, and are accordingly either for it, against it, or just tired
of hearing about it.

There will be others for whom 'training' is something you
do at the gym or at theological college or seminary, but who
have never considered that 'training' ought to happen in the
local church.

For the benefit of both groups, and all those in between,
let's pause to consider what 'training' really is in connection
with Christian life and ministry.

What is training?

A perennial difficulty in discussing 'training' (and many other
subjects) is that the word has connotations in English that don't
always correspond with how the word is used in the Bible.

In modern English, 'training' normally relates to becoming
proficient in some practice or art or profession. By a mix of
instruction, observation, practice and discipline, 'trainees'
learn how to do something well—whether that's running
hurdles or becoming a soldier. 'Training' in our world is usually
task-oriented, with a focus on the processes by which things get

done. It emphasizes uniform and predictable responses that are learnt and reinforced by practice. When we undertake 'workplace training', we hope that the outcome will be a new level of proficiency in some aspect of our role.

Ministry training can be like this as well—providing knowledge and skills so that Christians can learn how to do certain things. Along this line, many churches run 'training courses' to help people become more proficient at reading their Bibles, or sharing their faith with others, or welcoming newcomers, or leading small groups, and so on.

This is good and useful, but it's not the essence of 'training'— at least not in the way the Bible thinks about it. In the New Testament, training is much more about Christian thinking and living than about particular skills or competencies. We see this in the pastoral epistles, in the words that are translated as 'training' in our Bibles.

Imparting doctrine and life

In 1 Timothy 4:7, for example, we find this instruction from Paul: "Have nothing to do with irreverent, silly myths. Rather train yourself for godliness." The Greek word here is *gymnazō*, a word originally used in connection with athletics and contests. As a Christian minister, Timothy was to apply this metaphor of athletic training to his life and character, so that he and his hearers might progress towards maturity and righteousness. In Hebrews we find the same Greek word used in a similar way: "...solid food is for the mature, for those who have their powers of discernment trained by constant practice to distinguish good from evil" (Heb 5:14). By contrast, false teachers have their hearts "trained in greed" (2 Pet 2:14). The focus here is on teaching and example, leading to a particular character of life rather than to a particular skill or competency.

In 2 Timothy 3:16, the Greek word *paideia* is also translated as 'training': "All Scripture is breathed out by God and profitable for teaching, for reproof, for correction, and for *training* in righteousness". This is the normal word for instruction or teaching intended to form proper patterns of behaviour (in this case, righteousness). It's the same sort of training a father exercises over a son to mould his character—whether that's God as our Father who disciplines us for our good (Heb 12:5, 7) or our human fathers who seek to train us in ways of the Lord (Eph 6:4).

In the very next verse (2 Tim 3:17), the training concept is developed further. By being 'trained' in righteousness, the man of God is made competent or proficient by the Scriptures, which equip him for every good work. It's the 'training' in righteousness that leads to the proficiency, but the proficiency here is not a particular skill—such as being able to teach clearly, or lead a small group, or whatever—but a quality of character and behaviour based on the sound doctrine of the Scriptures.

The sound doctrine is vital. In the pastorals, a baton is being passed as in a relay—and that baton is the gospel itself. God entrusts the gospel to Paul (1 Tim 1:11-12), who in turn passes it on to Timothy (1 Tim 1:18-19; 6:11-14, 20-21). Paul now wants Timothy to do the same: to entrust what Paul has delivered to him to faithful people who will also be able to teach others (2 Tim 2:2).

The heart of training is not to impart a skill, but to impart sound doctrine. Paul uses the language of 'training' to refer to a lifelong process whereby Timothy and his congregation are taught by Scripture to reject false religion, and to conform their hearts and their lives to sound doctrine. Good biblical training results in a godly life based on sound, health-giving teaching.

Relationship and imitation
However, this transfer of the "good deposit" of the gospel is not a barren, educational exercise. It's deeply and inescapably

relational. When we look at the relationship between Paul and Timothy, it becomes immediately apparent that much more than a transfer of skills or information was involved in Timothy's training. Paul repeatedly describes Timothy with great warmth as his son and beloved child (1 Cor 4:17; Phil 2:22; 1 Tim 1:2, 18; 2 Tim 1:2) and as a fellow-believer and sharer in grace (1 Tim 1:2; 2 Tim 1:2, 2:1). Timothy was almost certainly converted through Paul's ministry (Acts 14:6-23, 16:1-3), and became a highly valued co-worker in the gospel mission ("I have no-one like him"—Phil 2:20), whom Paul trusted to send as his emissary to the churches (Phil 2:19-20; 1 Thess 3:1-5).

This close relationship was a vehicle for one of the key elements of Paul's training of Timothy—imitation. "You, however, have followed my teaching, my conduct, my aim in life, my faith, my patience, my love, my steadfastness, my persecutions and sufferings that happened to me at Antioch, at Iconium, and at Lystra—which persecutions I endured; yet from them all the Lord rescued me" (2 Tim 3:10-11).

It was not only the good deposit of the gospel that Paul passed on to Timothy, but a *way of life*. And Timothy was, in turn, to model this gospel way of living to others: "Let no one despise you for your youth, but set the believers an example in speech, in conduct, in love, in faith, in purity" (1 Tim 4:12). Paul exhorted one of his other protégés, Titus, along similar lines: "Show yourself in all respects to be a model of good works, and in your teaching show integrity, dignity, and sound speech that cannot be condemned, so that an opponent may be put to shame, having nothing evil to say about us" (Titus 2:7-8). Notice that Titus' exemplary teaching and behaviour reflects on Paul as well ("nothing evil to say about *us*"), because Titus was only teaching and behaving in imitation of Paul.

This methodology of modelling, example and imitation was basic to Paul's whole ministry:

Brothers, join in imitating me, and keep your eyes on those who walk according to the example you have in us. (Phil 3:17)

I do not write these things to make you ashamed, but to admonish you as my beloved children. For though you have countless guides in Christ, you do not have many fathers. For I became your father in Christ Jesus through the gospel. I urge you, then, be imitators of me. That is why I sent you Timothy, my beloved and faithful child in the Lord, to remind you of my ways in Christ, as I teach them everywhere in every church. (1 Cor 4:14-17)

Give no offense to Jews or to Greeks or to the church of God, just as I try to please everyone in everything I do, not seeking my own advantage, but that of many, that they may be saved. Be imitators of me, as I am of Christ. (1 Cor 10:32-11:1)

For we know, brothers loved by God, that he has chosen you, because our gospel came to you not only in word, but also in power and in the Holy Spirit and with full conviction. You know what kind of men we proved to be among you for your sake. And you became imitators of us and of the Lord, for you received the word in much affliction, with the joy of the Holy Spirit, so that you became an example to all the believers in Macedonia and in Achaia. (1 Thess 1:4-7)

The chain of imitation flows from the Lord Jesus himself, whom Paul is copying, through to Timothy (who models himself on Paul, and reminds others of Paul's ways), and to the believers, who become "imitators of us and of the Lord".

It is worth stressing that Paul wants them to imitate not only his doctrine but also his way of life. Paul never abstracts ethics from doctrine, because a right understanding of the gospel always leads to a changed life. We might cringe at this, from either a pious humility or an honest assessment of the poverty of our example. But Paul showed no embarrassment for himself or his co-workers. He urged Timothy and the others to join him in setting an example for the believers, and he urged the believers to follow it!

However, we must remember what sort of example it was that Paul was setting in his imitation of Jesus. It was the acceptance of hostility and social rejection—an embracing of the self-sacrificial path of suffering and mistreatment for the sake of others. As Edwin Judge argues, the kind of imitation Paul called for was quite counter-cultural in his day. It didn't consist of following particular ethical rules or traditions in imitation of one's spiritual master, but of giving up one's life for others. This "call to sacrifice one's own reasonable interest to a higher objective was a bewildering upending of the ethical life as the Greeks had refined it".[1]

Paul urged his congregations to join him in suffering for the mission of Christ, to seek the salvation of others by forgoing their own rights. His ambition to save others was to be their ambition too.

We are always an example to those whom we are teaching and training, whether we like it or not. We cannot stop being an example. One of the key tasks for pastors and elders is to frame their lives so that they serve as a godly model for others—which is why most of the requirements laid down for elders in places like 1 Timothy 3 and Titus 1 relate to character and lifestyle. It's not as if we are to model perfection—that would be impossible. But, as Paul says to Timothy, "Practice these things, immerse yourself in them, so that all may see your *progress*" (1 Tim 4:15). We are to set an example in *striving* for holiness, not in displaying perfectly achieved holiness (Heb 12:14). In fact, at the most profound level, the example we set is in modelling the way of the cross. We are not attempting to create clones or a cult of personality, but following our Master's example in persevering in the face of trials and persecution. If the teacher suffers, so also does the student.

The important point here is that training is inescapably relational. It cannot be done in a classroom via the supposedly neutral transferral of information. The trainer is calling upon the trainee to adopt not only his teaching, but also the way of life that necessarily flows from that teaching. And so the trainer must do as Paul instructed Timothy:

> Keep a close watch on yourself and on the teaching.
> Persist in this, for by so doing you will save both
> yourself and your hearers. (1 Tim 4:16)

Training as parenthood
We could summarize the Pauline model of ministry training by saying that it looks a lot like parenthood:

- It begins as someone is instrumental in bringing someone else to new birth.
- It is long term and loving.
- It includes passing on knowledge, wisdom and practical instruction.
- It involves modelling and imitation.
- It forms not only beliefs and abilities, but also character and lifestyle.

This is a very useful metaphor to keep in our minds as we think about training. Training is parenting. It's loving someone enough to want to see him or her grow and flourish, and being prepared to put in the long-term, faithful work that will (in God's mercy) see that happen.

The relational nature of training means that the best training will often occur by osmosis rather than formal instruction. It will be caught as much as it is taught. Trainees will end up resembling their trainers, much as children turn out like their parents.

In relational training, the hearts of both trainer and trainee are exposed. As we train ministers of Christ's word, we don't measure progress simply by the performance of tasks, but by the integrity of the heart. Does the trainee genuinely love God and his neighbour? Does he truly submit to Christ's word? Unguarded, spontaneous words and actions expose the heart of the trainee—the good, the bad and the ugly. In the cut and thrust of life and ministry the relationship is deepened, and the trainer gains insights into the character of the trainee.

Trainees likewise need to see into the heart of their trainers—the sins and confessions, the fears and faith, the visions and realities, the successes and failures. The life and ministry of the trainer is a model for the trainee—not of perfection but of godly desires in an earthen vessel. This requires an honest, open sharing of our lives.

Nowhere is this seen more clearly than in the home. In the home, the trainer is no longer the 'public Christian', the ministry leader. The persona drops away. He becomes—indeed he *is*—the husband laughing with his wife, the father dealing with his daughter not eating her food, the cook enjoying his creative side, the homemaker fixing the tap, the exhausted man gazing blankly at the TV. He is living out life in the Spirit in the hardest context. And in the same way, when a wise trainer is in the home of the trainee he is also observing how the trainee listens respectfully to his wife, or ignores the children, or expects to be waited upon, or can't relax. All this is relevant for later reflection and discussion.

Having said all this, it is also important to say that formal training will be an invaluable and irreplaceable complement to relational training. True, we may be aware of that rare trainer who can intuitively judge what is needed in the development of each trainee, and provide it on the fly. The intuitive trainer may not need to reflect very much about a formal training curriculum, so naturally does training come to him. But most of us aren't brilliantly intuitive trainers. And even those who are often fail to be comprehensive in their training. They have no idea what has been covered or not covered.

Formal training programs are not incompatible with relational training. If a trainer is committed to a relational approach, training programs enhance rather than detract from the personal training. In fact, formal training sessions or programs are another opportunity for the trainer to see the trainee in action—relating to people, participating, completing set tasks, and so on.

All of which leads us to the place of skills and courses in training.

What about skills, courses and programs?

Perhaps with the biblical emphasis firmly in the right place—on the training of mind and heart and character by the word of God—we are now ready to talk about skills or competencies in training.

The Bible does talk about practical abilities. All Christians, for example, should be "prepared to make a defence to anyone who asks you for a reason for the hope that is in you" (1 Pet 3:15), and ought to "consider how to stir one another up to love and good works" (Heb 10:24). It is also essential that some have the ability to teach—for example, the overseers in 1 Timothy 3:2, or the elders in Titus 1:9, or the "faithful men" in 2 Timothy 2:2. We are also told that some have gifts of 'leading' in Romans 12:8 (cf. those who 'manage' in 1 Timothy 3:4).

Skills and competencies are not irrelevant. In fact, they are necessary for communicating the gospel message, shepherding God's people and leading the church. However, skills must never be separated from the gospel—from the truth of sound doctrine, and the godly character that accords with it. It's very easy to get carried away with 'competencies'—to think that if only we get the skills and techniques right then everything will fall into place, and growth will be assured. It's easy to focus on skills as an end in themselves, and to put too much trust in them.

However, if we keep the gospel first and central, then learning to do particular activities more effectively can simply be a godly part of our service of Christ and other people. We can desire to become a better Bible teacher, for example, not out of self-glorification, or a misplaced trust in our own importance, but simply because we want to communicate the life-changing message of the Bible more clearly and compellingly to our hearers. And the same, of course, is true of our plans to train others in particular skills.

The nature and goal of training can be very usefully summarized by three Cs. Through personal relationship, prayer, teaching, modelling and practical instruction, we want to see people grow in:

- **conviction**—their knowledge of God and understanding of the Bible
- **character**—the godly character and life that accords with sound doctrine
- **competency**—the ability to prayerfully speak God's word to others in a variety of ways.

With a more biblical perspective about the nature of 'training' under our belts, we're in a better position to make use of the large variety of training courses and resources that are now available. If we remember that training is inescapably personal and relational, that it involves teaching and modelling sound doctrine *and* a way of life *and* the ability to serve others, then structures for training can be very useful indeed—whether we are talking about formal training programs, like the two-year apprenticeship model developed by the Ministry Training Strategy (MTS; more on this in chapter 11), or the various short training courses produced by Matthias Media, the publishers of this book (see appendix 2 for a list).

These programs and packages can provide a very helpful framework for training, so long as the structures and resources provided aren't seen as a replacement for the real work of personal training and modelling. Take a short training course like Matthias Media's *Six Steps to Encouragement*, for example. This is a six-week program (with DVD input and a booklet for each participant), which deals with the basics of personal ministry—of how one Christian can encourage another. It's the kind of thing a small home Bible study group would very usefully do as part of their regular pattern, or that a church would put on as a special training course over six Monday nights.

Now the temptation is simply to 'run the course'—by directing your small groups to do it, or by issuing a general invitation for interested people to sign up. And having run a group or groups of people through the course, you can pat yourself on the back for having done some 'training'. And there is no question that working through this material will be of benefit to those involved.

However, to make real progress in helping the Christians in your congregation become 'encouragers', they need more than a six-week course. They need the example of seeing it done; and they need the personal instruction and mentoring and prayer that addresses the spiritual issues at the heart of becoming an 'encourager'. This takes time and personal attention—before, during and after the structured training opportunity.

How might such a thing happen in the life of a busy pastor and his congregation? We will look at this in the chapters to follow, but first we need to lay down some other groundwork.

Endnote

1. EA Judge, 'The Teacher as Moral Exemplar in Paul and in the Inscriptions of Ephesus', in D Peterson and J Pryor (eds), *In the Fullness of Time: Biblical Studies in Honour of Archbishop Donald Robinson*, Anzea, Homebush West, NSW, 1992, p. 199.

Chapter 7

Training and gospel growth

The biblical idea of training we've been exploring so far assumes that gospel work is a 'growth industry'—that when the gospel is preached, and the Spirit is at work, then 'growth' is what happens.

We see this in Paul's warm greeting to the Colossians:

> "We always thank God, the Father of our Lord Jesus
> Christ, when we pray for you, since we heard of your
> faith in Christ Jesus and of the love that you have for all
> the saints, because of the hope laid up for you in
> heaven. Of this you have heard before in the word of the
> truth, the gospel, which has come to you, as indeed in
> the whole world it is bearing fruit and growing—as it
> also does among you, since the day you heard it and
> understood the grace of God in truth..." (Col 1:3-6)

The growth Paul has in mind here seems to have two facets. At one level, the gospel is growing throughout the world like a vine whose tendrils keep spreading across the fence, and over the fence, and into the neighbour's backyard. Even in Colossae, where Paul has never been, the gospel has been taught (by the noble Epaphras) and has taken root.

But it's also growing in another sense—in people's lives.

Where the "word of truth" is taught and believed, it bears fruit. People are changed. They are transferred from one kingdom to another (as Paul later puts it in verse 13). They begin to have a faith in Christ Jesus and a love for all the saints, and to long for their heavenly inheritance. Their priorities change, their world view changes, and their lives, bit by bit, are remade in the image of God's own Son. This is what Paul prays would keep happening in the lives of the Colossians: "And so, from the day we heard, we have not ceased to pray for you, asking that you may be filled with the knowledge of his will in all spiritual wisdom and understanding, so as to walk in a manner worthy of the Lord, fully pleasing to him, bearing fruit in every good work and increasing in the knowledge of God" (Col 1:9-10).

Now presumably there is nothing very shocking or revolutionary in these ideas. The gospel by its very nature produces growth. We all know that. However, there are three very important implications of this simple idea.

The *first* is that the growth of the gospel happens in the lives of people, not in the structures of my church. Or to put it in terms of our opening metaphor, the growth of the trellis is not the growth of the vine. We may multiply the number of programs, events, committees and other activities that our church is engaged in; we may enlarge and modernize our buildings; we may re-cast our regular meetings to be attractive and effective in communicating to our culture; we may congratulate ourselves that numbers are up. And all of these are good things! But if *people* are not growing in their knowledge of God's will so that they walk ever more worthily of the Lord, seeking to please him in all things and bearing fruit in every good work, then there is no growth to speak of happening at all.

There are many ways to get more people along to your church. In fact, some of the largest churches in the world are the least faithful to the gospel and the Bible. The Bible itself warns us that people will congregate wherever there are teachers who are willing to tell them what they want to hear (2 Tim 4:3-4). Numerical or structural growth is not necessarily an indicator of *gospel* growth. (Mind you, numerical failure is not an indicator of gospel growth either—we are not suggesting that small churches inherently foster more gospel growth than larger ones!)

Secondly, this means that we must be willing to lose people from our own congregation if that is better for the growth of the gospel. We must be happy to send members off to other places so that the gospel may grow there as well. And be warned: this will happen if you take gospel growth and training seriously. If you pour your time into people, and mentor and train them, the consequence will often be that some of your best people—in whom you have invested countless hours—will leave you. They will go to the mission field. They will join a church-planting team in another part of your city. They will take a job in a different part of the country because the gospel need is so great there. They will undertake further training, perhaps at theological college or seminary. A commitment to the growth of the gospel will mean that we train people towards maturity not for the benefit of our own churches or fellowships but for the benefit of Christ's kingdom.

The *third* radical implication of this understanding of 'gospel growth' lies in the way we think about people. We see people not as cogs in our wheel, or as resources for our projects, but as individuals each at their own stage of gospel growth. And our goal for each person is that they advance, that they make progress, that they move one step forward from where they are now.

Let's think about this in more detail.

Stages in gospel growth

Thinking broadly, there are four basic stages in the growth of the gospel in someone's life. We might call them:

- Outreach
- Follow-up
- Growth
- Training

At the *outreach* stage, people come into contact with the word of truth for the first time. It might initially be through a conversation about some issue in their lives or in the world. But somehow, in some context (large or small), someone explains the gospel to them. The seed takes root, and in God's time and by his Spirit, it bears fruit.

Once people respond to the gospel message and put their faith in Christ, some sort of initial *follow-up* is needed to establish them in the faith and teach them the basics. Depending on their background and circumstances, this initial stage of becoming firm in the faith can take a few months or several years; but however long it takes, it is vital that *someone* is sticking with the new Christian to teach, care for, and pray for them.

Then follows the lifelong process of *growth* as a Christian disciple—growing in the knowledge of God and the godly character that flows from that knowledge. This process of growth is not a cakewalk. It's a straight and narrow path, like Christian's in *The Pilgrim's Progress*, with plenty of hills, valleys, enemies and sidetracks along the way. At various points in their walk along this road, Christians will get into trouble and will need particular help, counsel and prayer. A great sickness or trial may overtake them; a particular sin may start to get the better of them; a season of spiritual weakness or dryness may come upon them. In all of these circumstances—in both good times and bad—the formula for growth is the same: the ministry of the word and Spirit. As the Bible's truth is prayerfully spoken and applied and heard, and as the Spirit works within, growth occurs.

The fourth stage—*training*—is not a sequential one, as if it happens after the growth is all finished. (How could it, since we never stop growing?) In fact, the 'training' stage happens as part of Christian growth, because Christian maturity is not individualistic and self-focused—as if we have reached the pinnacle of Christlike godliness when we have a one-hour quiet time each day. To grow like Christ is to grow in love and a desire to serve and minister to others. *We are using the word 'training' to describe the growth of all Christians in conviction, character and competency, so that in love they might minister to others by prayerfully bringing the word of God to them—whether to non-Christians in outreach, new Christians in follow-up, or all other Christians in daily growth.* If every Christian is a potential vine-worker (see chapter 4), then 'training' is that stage of Christian growth in which people are equipped and mobilized and resourced and encouraged to do that work. It is that stage in which their growth in conviction (beliefs), character (godliness) and competencies (skills/abilities) leads them to minister effectively to others.

THE GOSPEL GROWTH PROCESS

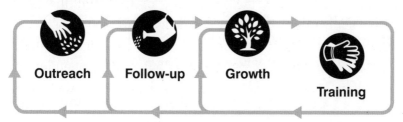

Now it is vital to remember two things. *Firstly*, while all Christians can and should be trained as vine-workers, not all will be gifted to minister in exactly the same way or to the same extent. Some will be preachers and teachers, others will be Bible study leaders, some will be very good at reaching out to non-Christians and answering their questions, others will focus on meeting one to one with new Christians and following them up, and still others will be fathers or mothers teaching their children. There are a myriad of contexts and opportunities for vine work, and each Christian will have his or her God-given part to play.

Secondly, training Christians to be vine-workers does not simply mean the impartation of certain skills and abilities (as we've already discussed at length above). Christian discipleship is about sound doctrine and a godly life, and so to train or equip someone to minister to others means training and equipping them with godliness and right thinking, not just with a set of skills—because that in turn is how they will need to minister to others. In order to follow up a new Christian, for example, a more mature believer needs not only to know how to run through a set of basic Bible studies; they also need to be able to model mature Christian faith and life.

Thinking about people

One enormous benefit of thinking about Christian growth in stages like this is that it helps us to think about, pray for and minister to people where they are at. If gospel growth really happens at the level of people's individual lives, how can we help each person move forward? How can we bring the word of God to bear for each one?

Here's a little diagnostic tool that will help us think about people. Jot down a list of seven people you know, both non-Christians and Christians in your church. Where is each of them up to in gospel growth? Let's see if we can visualize it by mapping out the various 'gospel growth' stages.[1]

	Outreach		Follow-up	Growth		Training	
	Raising issues	Gospel		Need help	Solid	General	Specific
Bob	•						
Jean				•			
Barry					•		
Tracey			•				
Don						•	
Mark		•					
Sarah							•

You'll notice that we've subdivided most of the stages to help our thinking.

Bob, for example, is not yet a Christian. He's definitely in the outreach stage, but in your discussions with him you haven't really got around to actually sharing the gospel with him. So far, it's been raising various issues that are connected with God and faith and the Bible, but it's early days. Mark, on the other hand, has come along to a guest service at church and has heard the gospel clearly explained. He still hasn't become a Christian, but he's further along than Bob.

Likewise, under the growth stage, you'll notice that Jean is in the 'need help' category whereas Barry is 'solid'. Both have been Christians for a number of years. Neither of them needs initial follow-up. But Jean is having a really tough time: her non-Christian husband has a gambling problem, and she is battling to raise her teenage kids virtually on her own. She has always been strong in faith, but in recent times has started to become bitter and angry with God, and been seen less often at church and Bible study group. Jean really needs help. She needs someone (or more than one person) to get alongside her, care for her, pray with her, encourage her from the Bible to keep going, and so on. Barry, on the other hand, is motoring along reasonably well. It's not all smooth sailing, of course, but at the moment he is making good, solid progress in the Lord.

Now, again, these are not simple, black-and-white, or strictly sequential categories. Nearly all Christians will move in and out of the 'need help' category at different points in their lives. Next year, it might be Barry's turn to go through the wringer. But for the sake of thinking through what each of them needs at the moment in order to grow in the gospel, it's useful to make a distinction.

In the training stage, there are also a couple of useful sub-categories: general and specific. These refer to equipping or training that is applicable to just about every Christian, and that which relates to specific ministries. Don, for example, is a solid mature Christian who is learning how to understand and share his faith with his non-Christian workmates. This is general training—it's something that all Christians should be equipped to do. Sarah, on the other hand, is a very capable and caring woman who has a real knack for explaining the Bible clearly. She is currently being trained to lead one of the women's Bible study groups that meet on Thursday mornings.

The point of using this sort of tool is not to turn Christian ministry into a set of lists but to help us *focus on people*—because ministry is about people, not programs. If we never think about people individually and work out where they are up to, and how and in what area they need to grow, how can we minister in anything other than a haphazard, scattergun way? It's like a doctor thinking to himself, "Seeing each of my patients individually and diagnosing their illnesses is just too difficult and time consuming. Instead, I'm going to get all my patients to assemble together each week, and I'll give them all the same medicine. I'll vary the medicine a bit from week to week, and it will at least do everybody some good. And it's much more efficient and manageable that way."

Some readers may suspect that this is starting to sound rather too anti-church and anti-sermon, and when you see the title of chapter 8 ('Why Sunday sermons are necessary but not sufficient'), your suspicions may get worse. We'll talk more about the issues in that chapter; suffice to say at this point that we are very pro-church and we think that the 'sermon' is an essential, valuable and highly effective form of ministering God's word— it's just that it's not the only form, nor the only way to see gospel growth happen. If growing the vine is about growing *people*, we need to help each person grow, starting from where they are at this very moment. There needs to be inefficient, individual people ministry, as well as the more efficient ministries that take place in larger groups. This is the sort of individualized ministry that Paul envisages in 1 Thessalonians 5:

> We ask you, brothers, to respect those who labour
> among you and are over you in the Lord and admonish
> you, and to esteem them very highly in love because of
> their work. Be at peace among yourselves. And we urge
> you, brothers, admonish the idle, encourage the
> fainthearted, help the weak, be patient with them all.
> (1 Thess 5:12-14)

The leaders labour hard in their vital role, and are to be esteemed highly because of it. But there is an equally important role for the "brothers" to be involved in: ministering to all the various situations that individual Christians encounter in life.

This is another enormous benefit of using a diagnostic tool like the one above. It helps us see what people need next— which is always to help them move one step to the right. What Need-Help-Jean needs next is to gain (or regain) her solidity and stability in Christian faith. What Solid-Barry needs next is some encouragement and training to start ministering to others, rather than just growing in his own happy world. What

Raising-Issues-Bob needs next is to get beyond discussing general issues of God or Christianity, and hear the gospel.

Incidentally, if you're the pastor of a church, this tool also helps you to see where the gaps and holes and needs are. In a healthy 'gospel growth' church, there should be a decent spread of people across all categories. If you list out all the people you know, both in your congregation and the contacts on the fringe of the congregation, you'll quickly see where the challenges are. If there are very few people in the outreach category, then your church is not doing enough to make contact with non-Christians and tell them the gospel. If there are lots in the outreach category but almost none in the follow-up category, there's every chance that you're running lots of events and programs to make contact with people, but not prayerfully sharing the gospel often enough so that people are actually converted and need to be followed up. And so on.

TRAINING IS THE ENGINE OF GOSPEL GROWTH. UNDER GOD, THE way to get more gospel growth happening is to train more and more mature, godly Christians to be vine-workers—that is, to see more people equipped, resourced and encouraged to speak the word prayerfully to other people, whether in outreach, follow-up or Christian growth.

Unfortunately, in most churches and for most pastors, hardly any effort goes into training. It's basically seen as the pastor's job to do the gospel growth, and since that is virtually impossible at a personal or individual level, it is all done at the general and large-group level. And before long, the management and running of events, groups, meetings and structures consumes the pastor's time and the church member's week.

There is another way. But before we talk more about what a training ministry looks like in practice, it's time to pause and deal with some issues that have no doubt been brewing in some readers' minds for some time.

Endnote

1. This diagnostic or planning table is shamelessly pinched and adapted from Peter Bolt's excellent little book *Mission Minded* (Matthias Media, Sydney, 2000).

Chapter 8

Why Sunday sermons are necessary but not sufficient

We've come to the point in the flow of our argument where we need to pause and consider in more detail how the model of training and growth we are proposing collides with the reality of our existing church structures and models and practices. Because collide it will. By far the greatest obstacle to rethinking and reforming our ministries is the inertia of tradition—whether the long-held traditions of our denominations and churchmanship, or the more recent traditions of the church growth movement that have become a kind of unspoken orthodoxy in many evangelical churches.

We will get to the somewhat alarming proposition contained in this chapter's title in due course, but first let's look at two very common approaches to pastoral ministry, and then contrast them with the approach of this book. Now of course these common approaches are stereotypes, and cannot reflect the multi-faceted reality of ministry in all its variety. All the same, we trust that you can recognize the structures and tendencies reflected in the descriptions, and make adjustments for your own situation accordingly.

There are three approaches or emphases we wish to examine, which we will call:

- the pastor as service-providing clergyman
- the pastor as CEO
- the pastor as trainer.

The pastor as service-providing clergyman

In this way of thinking about church life and ministry, the pastor's role is to care for and feed the congregation. In this sense, he is a professional clergyman (whether or not he is called a 'clergyman'), and there is an expectation on the part of both congregation and pastor that he is paid to fulfil certain core functions:

- to feed the flock through his Sunday sermons and administration of the sacraments
- to organize and run the Sunday gathering, which is seen as a time of worship for the congregation
- to put on various occasional services for different purposes, such as baptisms, weddings and possibly guest services
- to personally counsel congregation members, especially in times of crisis.

This is the classic Reformed-evangelical model of an ordained minister shepherding the flock given to him by Christ. And it has great strengths:

- It rightly puts regular preaching of the word at the centre of the ministry.
- It gathers the whole congregation as a family on Sunday for prayer, praise and preaching.
- The occasional services provide opportunities for outreach.
- The pastor cares for his people in times of crisis.

However, there are also very real (and obvious) disadvantages with this approach. For a start, the ministry that takes place in the congregation will be limited to the gifts and capacity of the pastor: how effectively he preaches, and how many people he can personally know and counsel. In this model, it becomes very difficult for the congregation to grow past a given ceiling (usually between 100 and 150 regular members).

Perhaps the most striking disadvantage of this way of thinking about ministry is that it feeds upon and encourages the culture of 'consumerism' that is already rife in our culture. It perfectly fits the spirit of our age whereby we pay trained professionals to do everything for us rather than do it ourselves—whether cleaning our car, ironing our shirts, or walking our dog. The tendency is for Christian life and fellowship to be reduced to an hour and a quarter on Sunday morning, with little or no relationship, and very little actual ministry taking place by the congregation themselves. In this sort of church culture, it becomes very easy for the congregation to think of church almost entirely in terms of 'what I get out of it', and thus to slip easily into criticism and complaint when things aren't to their liking.

Even the good practice of pastoral counselling can become focused on 'me' being cared for by the pastor—such that if the assistant minister visits instead, this is not seen as adequate: "The pastor only sent him because he couldn't be bothered coming himself".

None of this is simply to blame the 'consumer'! For all its historic strengths, the professional pastor-as-clergyman approach speaks loud and clear to church members that they are there to receive rather than to give. As a model, it tends to produce spiritual consumers rather than active disciples of Christ, and very easily gets stuck in maintenance mode. Outreach or evangelism, both for individual congregation members and the church as a whole, is down the list.

In many respects, this first way of thinking about pastoral ministry reflects the culture and norms of a different world—

the world of 16th- and 17th-century Christianized nations, in which the whole community was in church, and in which the pastor was one of the few with sufficient education to teach.

The pastor as CEO

In many respects, the 'church growth movement' of the 1970s and 80s was a direct response to the traditional Reformed-evangelical view of ministry and church life. People saw some of the disadvantages that we've outlined and began to think about how they could be addressed. Speaking in very broad generalizations, the result was a number of key shifts:

- The pastor was still the professional clergyman, but his role became more focused on leading the congregation as an organization with particular goals; he was still a preacher and a pastoral service-provider, but he was also now a managerial leader responsible for making all these things happen on a larger scale. If there was going to be growth, then the pastor had to learn the difference between running a corner shop as a sole trader and managing a department store with numerous staff and a range of services.
- The focus of Sunday shifted towards an 'attractional' model, with the kind of music, decor and preaching that would be attractive to visitors and newcomers. If the church was to grow, its 'shopfront' needed to be much more appealing to the 'target market'. It sounds tawdry when put like this, but for many churches it was profoundly gospel-centred. It stemmed from a godly desire to remove unnecessary cultural obstacles to the hearing of God's word, and to make sure that the only thing weird, offensive or strange about church was the gospel itself.
- Instead of occasional services, the church growth movement spawned a revolution of programs and events,

both for church members and for outsiders—everything from evangelistic courses and programs, to outreach events designed to be attractive to the non-Christian friends of the congregation, to seminars and programs to help congregation members with different aspects of their lives (how to raise children, how to deal with depression, and so on).

- In a church of 500 (rather than 150), how could individual members be known, cared for, prayed for and helped in times of crisis? Individual counselling by pastoral staff (let alone the senior pastor) was logistically impossible, especially given the range of other programs and activities happening. The answer was the rise of the small home group, in which members could have a set of personal relationships in which they could be known and cared for.

One of the key strengths and advantages of the church growth approach has been its promotion of congregational *involvement*. This is one of the key insights of the movement—that if you want someone to join your congregation and feel part of the place, they need to have something to do. Church growth research told us that if you found someone a role or job or opportunity for personal involvement in some ministry within the first six months of them being at your church, then your chances of retaining that person as a long-term member massively improved.

The other key strength of the 'church growth' approach is its recognition that if a congregation is to grow numerically, more work will need to be put into the trellis. As the cliché goes, the pastor will have to spend less time 'in the business' and more time 'on the business'. This is simply an inevitable function of organizational growth and change, and 'church growth' thinking has helped many pastors to face these challenges of leadership.

There is no doubt that many churches have grown in the past 30 years through successfully applying 'church growth' principles. It has enabled churches to grow past 150, and to promote a more active involvement of congregation members in various church groups, activities and programs.

The downside has been that for all the growth in numbers and involvement, many 'church growth' churches have also accepted the consumerist assumptions of our society. Success has been achieved by providing a more attractive and broadly appealing 'product', but the result is not always more prayerful ministry of the word, and thus more real spiritual growth. Lots of people are involved and cared for and receiving help in their lives, but are people growing as disciples and in mission?

Willow Creek Community Church recently discovered this after 20 years at the forefront of the church growth movement. In a detailed survey of their members, the Willow Creek staff discovered that despite running one of the slickest and most well-organized churches in America—with superb structures, high-quality music and drama, and an impressive level of involvement of members in all manner of small groups and activities—personal spiritual growth as disciples was not happening.[1]

We could represent these two approaches in a table like this:

	Pastor as clergyman	Pastor as CEO
Pastor is...	preacher and service-provider	preacher and manager
Sunday is...	service of worship	attractional meeting
Outside of Sunday...	occasional services	range of events and programs
Pastoral care through...	counselling and visitation	small groups
Church is like...	a small corner store with one employee	a department store with numerous staff
Tends to result in...	consumers in maintenance mode	consumers in growth mode

The pastor as trainer

We have been arguing from the Bible that:

- genuine spiritual growth only comes as the Holy Spirit applies the word of God to people's hearts
- all Christians have the privilege and responsibility to prayerfully speak the word of God to each other and to non-Christians, as the means by which God gives this growth.

If these two foundational propositions are true, then we need a different mental picture of church life and pastoral ministry—one in which the prayerful speaking of the word is central, *and* in which Christians are trained and equipped to minister God's word to others. Our congregations become centres of training where people are trained and taught to be disciples of Christ who, in turn, seek to make other disciples.

- In this way of thinking, the pastor is a prayerful preacher who shapes and drives the entire ministry through his biblical, expositional preaching. This is essential and foundational. But crucially, the pastor is also a trainer. His job is not just to provide spiritual services, nor is it his job to do all of the ministry. His task is to teach and train his congregation, by his word and his life, to become disciple-making disciples of Jesus. There is a radical dissolution, in this model, of the clergy-lay distinction. It is not minister and ministered-to, but the pastor and his people working in close partnership in all manner of word ministries.
- Adding this training emphasis greatly enhances what we do in our Sunday gatherings, because it builds and grows the gospel maturity of those who attend. We are training people to be contributors and servants, not spectators and consumers. The congregation becomes a gathering of

disciple-making disciples in the presence of their Lord—meeting with him, listening to his word, responding to him in repentance and worship and faith, and discipling one another. The congregational gathering becomes not only a theatre for ministry (where the word is prayerfully spoken) but also a spur and impetus for the worship and ministry that each disciple will undertake in the week to come.

- Where the pastor is a trainer, there will be a focus on people ministering to people, rather than on structures, programs and events. Evangelism will take place as disciples reach out to the people around them: in their homes, their extended families, their streets, their workplaces, their schools, and so on. Events and programs and guest services will still be useful structures to focus people's efforts and provide opportunities to invite friends, but the real work of prayerful evangelism will take place as the disciples do it themselves. Taking our example from the previous chapter, it will happen as Don takes the time to get to know Bob, and then offers to read through one of the Gospels with him.

- Pastoral care, in this approach, is also founded on disciples being trained to care for and disciple other Christians. Small groups may be utilized as one convenient structure in which this may happen, but the structure itself will not make it happen. Our goal should not simply be to 'get people into small groups'. Unless Christians are taught and trained to meet with each other, to read the Bible and pray with each other, and to urge and spur one another on to love and good works, the small-group structure will not be effective for spiritual growth. People may get to know each other in small groups, feel a sense of togetherness and community, develop warm friendships, and be more bound in to regular attendance and involvement in the church as a result—but none of these things amounts to growth in the gospel. It's very possible for a great deal of the personal encouragement and discipling work in a congregation to be done one to one, without any involvement in structured small groups.[2]

The 'pastor-as-trainer' approach contrasts with our other two models like this:

	Pastor as clergyman	Pastor as CEO	Pastor as trainer
Pastor is…	preacher and service-provider	preacher and manager	preacher and trainer
Sunday is…	service of worship	attractional meeting	gathering of worshipping disciples with their Lord
Outside of Sunday…	occasional services	range of events and programs	disciples reaching out to make disciples
Pastoral care through…	counselling and visitation	small groups	people ministering to people
Church is like…	a small corner store with one employee	a department store with numerous staff	a team with an active captain-coach
Tends to result in…	consumers in maintenance mode	consumers in growth mode	disciples in mission mode

At this point, it is worth repeating the caveats made earlier in this chapter (in case they have faded from memory). We are unavoidably dealing with straw men and stereotypes in this discussion. No particular church will be a perfect example of any one of these approaches or emphases; there will be massive individual variation. Indeed, you may look at your own congregation and recognize it as a strange amalgam of two or more!

All the same, as a thought experiment, delineating these three approaches is helpful. The tendencies and traditions are recognizable, as are the consequences.

The insufficient sermon

Perhaps the best way to sharpen what we are arguing for in this chapter is to say that Sunday sermons are necessary but not sufficient. This may sound like heresy to some of our readers, and in one sense we hope it does sound a bit shocking. Are we de-valuing preaching? Surely godly, faithful expository sermons accompanied by prayer are all that is really required for the building of Christ's church?

Sermons are needed, yes, but they are not *all* that is needed. Let's be absolutely clear: the preaching of powerful, faithful, compelling biblical expositions is absolutely vital and necessary to the life and growth of our congregations. Weak and inadequate preaching weakens our churches. As the saying goes, 'sermonettes produce Christianettes'. Conversely, clear, strong, powerful public preaching is the bedrock and foundation upon which all other ministry in the congregation is built. The sermon is a rallying call. It is where the whole congregation can together feed on God's word and be challenged, comforted and edified. The public preaching ministry is like a framework that sets the standard and agenda for all the other word ministries that take place. We do not want to see less emphasis on preaching or less effort go into preaching! On the contrary, we long for more godly, gifted Bible teachers who will set congregations on fire with the power of the preached word.

To say that sermons (in the sense of Bible expositions in our

Sunday gatherings) are necessary but not sufficient is simply to stand on the theological truth that it is the word of the gospel that is sufficient, rather than any one particular form of its delivery. We might say that the speaking of the word of the gospel under the power of the Spirit is entirely sufficient—it's just that on its own, the 25-minute sermonic form of it is not.

We say this because the New Testament compels us to. As we have already seen, God expects all Christians to be disciple-makers by prayerfully speaking the word of God to others—in whatever way and to whatever extent that their gifting and circumstances allow. When God has gifted all the members of the congregation to help grow disciples, why should we silence the contribution of all but one of them (the pastor), and think that this is sufficient or acceptable?

In his fine book on preaching, *Speaking God's Words*, Peter Adam conducts a detailed survey of the ministries of the word in the New Testament, together with a consideration of the ministry practices of John Calvin, Richard Baxter and ministries in our churches today. He concludes that:

> ...while preaching... is one form of the ministry of the Word, many other forms are reflected in the Bible and in contemporary Christian church life. It is important to grasp this point clearly, or we shall try and make preaching carry a load which it cannot bear; that is, the burden of doing all that the Bible expects of every form of ministry of the Word.[3]

Adam goes on to define preaching as the "the explanation and application of the Word to the congregation of Christ in order to produce corporate preparation for service, unity of faith, maturity, growth and upbuilding".[4] But he points out that Sunday preaching is not the only way to address the edification of the body:

While individuals may be edified in so far as they are members of the congregation, there may well be other areas in which they need correction and training in righteousness which they will not obtain through the Sunday sermon, because by its very nature it is generalist in its application.[5]

Well, you may ask, what is being suggested—that as well as a 25-minute sermon, we have 50 one-minute testimonies from the congregation?

That might make for a fascinating and encouraging (if rather long) Sunday morning, but that is not what we're proposing. Because Sunday is not the only place where the action is. This is something that one of the great gospel ministers of our Reformed-evangelical heritage knew very well.

The example of Richard Baxter

The name of Richard Baxter will forever be associated with his classic work *The Reformed Pastor*. Interestingly, by 'Reformed', Baxter did not mean a particular brand of doctrine (although his own somewhat idiosyncratic theology was certainly 'Reformed' in that sense), but rather a ministry that was renewed and renovated, and that abounded in vigour, zeal and purpose. "If God would but reform the ministry," Baxter wrote, "and set them on their duties zealously and faithfully, the people would certainly be reformed".[6]

Baxter's remarkable ministry among the 800 families of the village of Kidderminster began in 1647, and transformed the parish. His strategy of pastoral ministry was formed during the chaotic vacuum of ecclesiastical authority and discipline following the English Civil War and the failure of the Westminster reforms. Baxter wanted to ensure that every parishioner understood the basic tenets of the faith and the godly life, and *The Reformed Pastor*, published in 1656, consists of an extended exhortation to his fellow ministers to conduct a ministry that is not merely formal, but personal and local.

In calling for this reformation of ministry and church life, Baxter's chief motive was the salvation of souls: "We are seeking to uphold the world, to save it from the curse of God, to perfect the creation, to attain the ends of Christ's death, to save ourselves and others from damnation, to overcome the devil, and demolish his kingdom, to set up the kingdom of Christ, and to attain and help others to the kingdom of glory".[7]

This overriding and confronting challenge to the conversion of souls permeates each section of *The Reformed Pastor*—whether speaking about the pastor's oversight of himself or his oversight of the flock. This, Baxter had come to believe, was the true cause and agenda for reformation of the church. It could not be achieved merely through structural changes:

> I can well remember the time when I was earnest for
> the reformation of matters of ceremony... Alas! Can we
> think that the reformation is wrought, when we cast out
> a few ceremonies, and changed some vestures, and
> gestures, and forms! Oh no, sirs! It is the converting
> and saving of souls that is our business. That is the
> chiefest part of reformation, that doth most good, and
> tendeth most to the salvation of the people.[8]

In Baxter's view, if the ministry was going to be reformed to focus on the conversion of souls, pastors had to devote extensive time to "the duty of personal catechizing and instructing the flock". He saw personal work with people as having irreplaceable value, because it provided "the best opportunity to impress the truth upon their hearts, when we can speak to each individual's particular necessity, and say to the sinner, 'Thou art the man'".[9] Public preaching was not enough, according to Baxter. In fact, he went so far as to say "I have no doubt that the Popish auricular confession is a sinful novelty... but our common neglect of personal instruction is much worse"![10] It was only through personal catechizing that Baxter could find those who:

> ...have been my hearers eight or ten years, who know not whether Christ be God or man, and wonder when I tell them the history of his birth and life and death as if they have never heard it before... I have found that some ignorant persons, who have been so long unprofitable hearers, have got more knowledge and remorse in half an hour's close discourse, than they did from ten years public preaching. I know that preaching the gospel publicly is the most excellent means, because we speak to many at once. But it is usually far more effectual to preach it privately to a particular sinner.[11]

Elsewhere, Baxter wrote:

> It is but the least part of the Minister's work, which is done in the Pulpit... To go daily from one house to another, and see how you live, and examine how you profit, and direct you in the duties of your families, and in your preparation for death, is the great work.[12]

Baxter worked hard to convince others of the need for this kind of ministry reformation. He formed the 'Worcester Association' to promote the cause, members of which embraced the commitment to know personally each person in their charge—a challenging commitment even now, but revolutionary in Baxter's time.

Sadly, however, Baxter's example was "widely hailed, less widely followed, and finally, perhaps more often than not, simply abandoned..."[13] Certainly, not many pastors today walk in his footsteps, even though they may have read *The Reformed Pastor* at some point in seminary and nodded approvingly. The *idea* of personal ministry alongside preaching ministry is admirable and hard to disagree with. It is also thoroughly biblical. Paul says to the Ephesian elders that he "did not shrink from declaring to you anything that was profitable, and teaching you in public and from house to house" (Acts 20:20). The location for word ministry is necessarily public, but it is also inescapably personal and domestic. According to Baxter, this is the only way we can fulfil Paul's powerful exhortation to those same elders: "Pay careful attention to yourselves and to all the flock, in which the Holy Spirit has made you overseers, to care for the church of God, which he obtained with his own blood" (Acts 20:28).

Given that our context is undeniably very different from Baxter's—culturally, politically, socially, educationally—how do his insights inform our understanding of ministry? There are four key challenges:

- Evangelism is at the heart of pastoral ministry. Ministry is not about just dealing with immediate crises or problems, or about building numbers, or about reforming structures. It is fundamentally about preparing souls for death.
- Ministers need not be tied to traditional structures but should use whatever 'means' (Baxter's term) available to call people to repentance and salvation. For Baxter, this meant not being tied to the pulpit, but also going into people's houses to instruct and exhort them.
- We should focus not only on what we are teaching, but also on what the people are learning and applying.
- In many respects, in our era of widespread education, there is even more scope to implement Baxter's vision of personal catechizing. In many parts of the world, there is now a highly-educated laity who can not only learn well, but also very ably teach others. The personal house-to-

house discipling can be done not only by the pastor, but also by the disciple-makers that the pastor trains.

One of the first steps in applying these challenges is to conduct an honest audit of all your congregational programs, activities and structures, and assess them against the criteria of gospel growth. How many of them are still useful vehicles for outreach, follow-up, growth or training? Is there duplication? Are some structures or regular activities long past their use-by date? Saying 'yes' to more personal ministry almost always means saying 'no' to something else.

However, even freeing up some time in the diary may still leave us feeling swamped with the amount of 'people work' there is to do. That's why we need co-workers.

Endnotes

1. See G Hawkins and C Parkinson, *Reveal: Where Are You?*, Willow Creek Resources, Chicago, 2007.
2. For further thinking about small groups and how they can be positive vehicles for gospel growth, see Colin Marshall, *Growth Groups*, Matthias Media, Sydney, 1995.
3. Peter Adam, *Speaking God's Words: A Practical Theology of Preaching*, IVP, Leicester, 1996, p. 59.
4. Adam, p. 71.
5. Adam, p. 71.
6. Richard Baxter, *Reliquiae Baxterianae*, ed. M Sylvester, London, 1696, p. 115, cited in JI Packer, *A Quest for Godliness*, Crossway Books, Wheaton, 1990, p. 38.
7. Richard Baxter, *The Reformed Pastor*, 5th edn, Banner of Truth, London, 1974, p. 112.
8. Baxter, *The Reformed Pastor*, p. 211.
9. Baxter, *The Reformed Pastor*, p. 175.
10. Baxter, *The Reformed Pastor*, pp. 179-80.
11. Baxter, *The Reformed Pastor*, p. 196.
12. Baxter, *The Saints' Everlasting Rest*, sig. A4, cited in J William Black, *Reformation Pastors: Richard Baxter and the Ideal of the Reformed Pastor*, Paternoster, Milton Keynes, 2004, p. 177.
13. Black, *Reformation Pastors*, p. 105.

Chapter 9 |

Multiplying gospel growth through training co-workers

Let's return to our inspired but overwhelmed pastor. He wants his church to become a training centre, and he wants to equip his people as 'vine-workers', but at the same time he is swamped with work—preaching, committees, pastoral crises, and all the rest. He has 130 people to take care of—regular attenders and various contacts and people on the fringe—and he goes through the exercise of listing them all down and assessing where they are up to in the 'gospel growth' process.

The problem is, he barely has time to spend with ten of them, let alone 130. How is he going to start ministering personally to this sort of number? How is he going to make progress in training them to be vine-workers?

Let's break the problem down by considering our seven imaginary people from the 'gospel growth' table in chapter 7.

	Outreach		Follow-up		Growth		Training	
	Raising issues	Gospel			Need help	Solid	General	Specific
Bob	•							
Jean					•			
Barry						•		
Tracey			•					
Don							•	
Mark		•						
Sarah								•

Now, say our pastor only has time to meet with two of them personally. Which two should he meet with?

We might say Jean (because she really needs help) and Bob (because he really needs to hear the gospel). Then again, we might say Mark (because he is close to crossing the line and becoming a Christian) and Tracey (because she has crossed the line and is in urgent need of follow-up). This leaves our more mature Christians (Barry, Don and Sarah) with no input from the pastor, but since they are pretty solid, we assume that they will cope.

However, the diary only has room for two people. So who's it going to be? In the end, most pastors would probably end up choosing Tracey and Jean, because they are members of the congregation and Christians, and the pastor may feel he owes it to them. He will have to leave Bob and Mark (the non-Christians) until some other time.

At one level, these sorts of decisions simply throw us back on the sovereignty of God. All Christian ministry is like this. There are more people than we can ever get to. It doesn't all depend on us, praise be to God!

However, in terms of making wisest use of his time and energies, and maximizing the possibilities of gospel growth, the people our pastor should really pour his time into are Don and Sarah, followed closely by Barry.

Don, remember, is already doing some training in how to share the gospel with others. If our pastor puts some time into helping and mentoring Don in this, then he can encourage Don to pray for and meet with Bob and Mark (the two non-Christians), perhaps to work through some evangelistic Bible studies together.

Sarah has the heart and the gifts; all she needs is some personal encouragement, instruction and mentoring, and she would be more than capable of getting next to Jean to encourage her, as well as doing some basic follow-up with Tracey.

So by putting his time into Don and Sarah, our busy pastor has also ministered (through them) to four others. That leaves Barry, and he is next on the list to do some training with.

This, it has to be said, is counter-intuitive. It goes against the grain. Our first instinct is to go straight to those who need the most help—and of course, as pastors, there will always be times when we need to leave the 99 to go after the one. There will be pastoral emergencies and problems that we just have to deal with.

But if we pour all our time into caring for those who need help, the stable Christians will stagnate and never be trained to minister to others, the non-Christians will stay unevangelized, and a rule of thumb will quickly emerge within the congregation: if you want the pastor's time and attention, get yourself a problem. Ministry becomes all about problems and counselling, and not about the gospel and growing in godliness.

And over time, the vine withers.

Paul's band of brothers

Of course, we are by no means the first to suggest that Christian ministry is a team game. The apostle Paul himself had a large network of colleagues and co-workers who worked alongside him in his ministry. Up to 100 names are associated with Paul in the New Testament, of which around 36 could be considered close partners and fellow labourers. Paul uses two names in particular for them: fellow workers (*sunergoi*) and ministers (*diakonoi*).

Without trying to slavishly reproduce the Pauline pattern, what can we learn from his example? Let's look at each of the two titles or designations.

Fellow workers

Paul characteristically speaks of himself as a labourer for Christ, a worker who toils and strives in the work that the Lord has given him to do (see, for example, 1 Corinthians 3:8-9, 16:10; Philippians 1:22; Colossians 1:29). The result of his ministry, such as the Corinthian church, he describes as his "workmanship in the Lord" (1 Cor 9:1).

It is natural enough, then, that Paul should refer to those who work alongside him as his *sunergoi*, his co-workers or fellow workers. In Romans 16, Prisca and Aquila are described as his "fellow workers in Christ Jesus", Urbanus is a "fellow worker in Christ" and Timothy is just a plain "fellow worker". Elsewhere, Timothy is also called "our brother and God's co-worker in the gospel of Christ" (1 Thess 3:2). The noble Epaphroditus is a "brother and fellow worker and fellow soldier" (Phil 2:25). And Paul wants Euodia and Syntyche to patch up whatever it is they are disagreeing about, because these women "have laboured side by side with me in the gospel together with Clement and the rest of my fellow workers, whose names are in the book of life" (Phil 4:2-3).

Paul's ministry was collegial. There is a brotherliness and unity to it that stems from their common status as fellow workers—not just with each other, but also with God:

> What then is Apollos? What is Paul? Servants through whom you believed, as the Lord assigned to each. I planted, Apollos watered, but God gave the growth. So neither he who plants nor he who waters is anything, but only God who gives the growth. He who plants and he who waters are one, and each will receive his wages according to his labour. For we are God's fellow workers. You are God's field, God's building. (1 Cor 3:5-9)

Their common status as God's labourers both dignifies and humbles. They are working alongside God in his great work in the world; and yet they are nothing, because it is God who gives the growth.

Ministers

Paul also uses the language of 'ministry' to refer to his fellow workers who labour alongside him and also act on his behalf. Paul and Apollos are both fellow workers; they are also both "servants" (or 'ministers'—*diakonoi* in the Greek), each being assigned their ministry by the Lord (1 Cor 3:5). Later in the letter to the Corinthians, the household of Stephanas is described in similar terms:

> Now I urge you, brothers—you know that the household of Stephanas were the first converts in Achaia, and that they have devoted themselves to the service [= 'ministry'] of the saints—be subject to such as these, and to every fellow worker and labourer. I rejoice at the coming of Stephanas and Fortunatus and Achaicus, because they have made up for your absence, for they refreshed my spirit as well as yours. Give recognition to such men. (1 Cor 16:15-18)

It's a lovely picture of mutual labour and encouragement. These early converts not only joined Paul in labouring for the gospel; they also travelled to meet him on behalf of the Corinthians, and to refresh his spirit.

In Colossians, we meet Epaphras, Paul's "beloved fellow servant", who is a "faithful minister of Christ"; having been the one who originally taught the Colossians the word of the gospel, and who now struggles in prayer on their behalf (Col 1:7, 4:12). This is the same gospel "of which I, Paul, became a minister" (Col 1:23).

We could go on. There is Tychicus, the faithful *diakonos* in the Lord (Eph 6:21; Col 4:7), and Archippus, who is exhorted to "fulfil the ministry that you have received in the Lord" (Col 4:17), not to mention Timothy, who is entrusted with the ministry of the gospel (1 Tim 1:18), and is exhorted to be a good minister of Christ by devoting himself at all times to preaching and teaching (1 Tim 4:6, 13), even when it is unpopular (2 Tim 4:1-5).

Two themes emerge as we consider the ministry of Paul's co-workers. Firstly, although they are sometimes the 'ministers of Paul'—that is, agents acting on Paul's behalf between himself and the churches—they are also the ministers of Christ. They are doing the work and bidding of the Lord, not just of Paul. Secondly, the ministry they undertake is not just any service or help, but a service that is related to the spread of the word and the building of the church.

Implications

We should hardly be surprised that Paul gathered a team around him for the cause of the gospel. If nothing else, his ecclesiology would have driven him to it. Paul valued the diverse gifts of grace supplied by the Spirit for the building of the body of Christ, and accordingly worked alongside a variety of associates in a diversity of roles, from preacher to scribe to messenger to prayer-warrior. Inevitably some of Paul's fellow workers were closer and more long term than others, but he treated them all as brothers and fellow workers. Paul had no disciples, for there is only one Master. Women were also integrally involved in Paul's team, hosting churches in their homes, providing patronage (like Phoebe in Romans 16:1-2), and contending alongside him for the advance of the gospel.

On the face of it, we would need good reasons *not* to adopt Paul's methodology of team ministry. Theologically, it is an expression of the character of the church as a body with many parts. Practically and strategically, it provides support, refreshment, a sharing of the burden, and a multiplication of effective gospel work.

Of course, much of Paul's mission was itinerant, and many of his fellow workers were involved in his evangelistic and church-planting ministry. But some were also the leaders and pastors of the churches. Here, too, the standard pattern seems to be plurality rather than singularity, whether that be a team of elders/overseers working in one congregation, or a college of elders associated with a cluster of house churches.

It is hard to avoid the conclusion that both the itinerant mission and the local congregational work were team operations. Yet somehow this vision has been lost in many churches, even within those whose history and tradition emphasizes a plurality of elders. Over time, the model of a single ordained minister working alone to pastor a church has become the norm, even though it is strikingly different from the normal pattern of ministry in the New Testament.

Now, before we get distracted by age-old debates about church polity and governance, that is not what we're talking about. There are plenty of Anglican rectors who assemble strong teams for ministry, just as there are plenty of Presbyterian teaching elders who labour virtually alone—and vice versa. The important principle is that a pastor should not and cannot attempt the task of ministering to a congregation on his own. We need co-workers.

We need people, in other words, like Don and Sarah and Barry (from our illustration above)—soundly converted people of Christian maturity who can work alongside us in evangelism, follow-up, growth and training others. Co-workers can be involved in many activities, both in doing them and in training and encouraging others to do them:

- personal evangelism and training others to share the gospel
- leading small groups and overseeing a network of small groups
- following up new Christians and training others to follow up new Christians
- leading youth groups and training the next generation of youth leaders
- meeting one to one with men or women, and training others to meet one to one.

Some of these co-workers may end up being paid by the congregation to work in these ministries—either full-time or part-time—and some will pay for themselves through secular work. Some may be officially recognized in your congregational structures (by being an 'elder', for example); others may not. Some may be officially recognized by your denomination (i.e. be 'ordained'); the vast majority will not.

Regardless of the structures, titles or recognition, the principle is simple: by far the best way to build a congregation full of disciple-making disciples is to assemble and train a band of co-workers to labour alongside you. When it is just you, with 120+ people needing to be evangelized, followed-up, nurtured and trained, it is just impossible—especially given all the structures, meetings, committees, programs and activities that church life seems to generate.

But what if you were to start by gathering just ten potential co-workers, meeting with them regularly, and training and exciting them about the possibilities for ministry together? You might do nothing else for a year but gather your co-workers together in your lounge room each week to pray for the congregation, to wrestle over the Scriptures, to discuss theology, to confess sins to each other, and to train them in different aspects of ministry. But at the end of that year, you would have a close-knit, single-minded team of gospel partners, ready and able to work alongside you in ministry.

Bruce Hall has been doing something like this for years at St Paul's, Carlingford, in Sydney's north-west. Here's how he explains his regular meetings with lay co-workers:

> Churches don't make disciples; disciples make disciples (Matt 28:19-20). The principle I follow with lay workers is: If we are not on the same page spiritually then we won't be on the same page in ministry. So:
>
> 1. I choose men to meet with me weekly from 6.30-7.30 am.
> 2. I used to do it Tuesday, Wednesday, and Thursday; these days only Tuesday.
> 3. We spend 15 minutes chatting, catching up. I lead for half an hour, just reading a section of the Bible and commenting and inviting comments and applications to us; then we have 15 minutes of prayer. Which Scripture we read is irrelevant.
> 4. We always focus on where we are up to in our witnessing, and occasionally we will just pray (and not read Scriptures).
> 5. I always have my wardens (elders) in the group and we have about 8-10 in each group.

Consequences:

1. Most of those in administration (wardens and parish councillors) have been in such a group with me.

2. Most of the other congregational ministers on staff here run similar groups. Consequently most of the home group leaders and other leaders have been in such 'breakfast' groups.

3. Guys in the group see me with all my strengths and weaknesses, hear me pray, see me read the Bible, and hear my passions and theological perspectives.

4. We seldom have 'relationship' issues when we are arguing about the business of the church or future directions, because we meet together to pray in the mornings.

5. The ministries they are involved in are lay pastoring (alongside the congregational minister), home group leadership, wardens, parish council, and just about everything else.

How to select co-workers

In one sense, the criteria for selecting co-workers are obvious. Co-workers need to be people who have a heart for God and a hunger to learn and grow. They need to be soundly converted, mature believers with some runs on the board in Christian living, who have the faithfulness and potential to minister to others. It's 2 Timothy 2:2—"and what you have heard from me in the presence of many witnesses entrust to faithful men who will be able to teach others also".

However, it's easy to make mistakes when recruiting fellow workers. Here are some blunders to avoid:

- **Compromising on core beliefs and values:** You have a person in your congregation who has been a Christian for some time, is warm and sincere, has obvious gifts and capacities, but thinks differently on some important areas of theology. They may have a charismatic understanding of the Spirit's work, for example, or a more liberal view of the authority of Scripture. To take this sort of person on as a co-worker almost guarantees division and damage to the ministry. A co-worker must be completely dependable in rightly handling the word of truth. You must be able to trust them to teach others.

- **Being impressed by flashiness over substance:** It's very easy to be dazzled by the enthusiast with the outgoing personality, the up-front skills, and the charisma to lead people. But it's far more important to look for someone who really loves and obeys Christ, who lives a godly and disciplined life, whose family life is exemplary, and who has a servant heart.

- **Ignoring their track record:** Does the person serve when they don't have a formal position? Do others respect them as godly disciples of Christ? If they are not a servant at heart now, are they ready to lead others?

- **Choosing those who aren't good at relating to people:** Is the person you're considering socially awkward, or dominating, or prickly? Do they put other people on edge? Do they have a sense of humour? Christian ministry is inescapably relational, and some people are just not gifted relationally.

- **Recruiting in desperation:** The burden of ministry is sometimes so heavy that you will be tempted to recruit *anybody* as a co-worker, just to ease the load. This is a big mistake. It's much better to keep your team small, tight, unified and effective than to pull people on board who aren't ready or right.

- **Selecting the unteachable:** Some people are doctrinaire and dogmatic, and just not willing to think or grow. You need people who have a hunger for the truth, who tremble before God's word and who want to conform their lives to the Scriptures.

- **Choosing 'yes' people:** It's always tempting to recruit our admirers and supporters, the people who make us feel good by always seeming to be on our side. But they may not be the right people.
- **Calling for volunteers:** Recruiting fellow workers is not like asking for a few people to stay behind and stack the chairs. It is something that must be done by personal invitation, after careful thought and prayer.

So much for what not to do.

Tips for training co-workers

Once we've selected some likely people, and we're sitting down with them—individually or as a group—how do we set the task before them? What are we inviting them to do?

At the most basic level, we're inviting them to give up their lives for the service of Christ. We're just inviting them to be disciples, in other words. We shouldn't undersell this! We're not asking people to contribute to a little club that they happen to be part of—as if we're trying to find someone to be the secretary of the local junior rugby club for the year. We're inviting people to join us in the most significant work in the world—the work that God is doing to gather people into his kingdom through the prayerful proclamation of the gospel of his Son. So we're recruiting people to be part of a cause that is worth giving their lives to, and we should set this vision before our potential co-workers in all its glory and grandeur.

And yet, it's also important that we outline what the specific goals and aims are for the next 12 months. The vision might be as big as heaven and earth, but the steps we're going to take along the path in front of us need to be visible and attainable.

This means giving people a clear understanding of what the time commitment will be, what preparation is involved, what training they will receive and what ministries might ensue.

For example, you might decide to run a two-hour fortnightly team meeting with six people in your congregation that you think have the potential to be co-workers. Your two hours could be structured like this:

Activity	Time guide
Bible study: led by you, or one of the team members; you could use this time to train people in how to lead Bible discussions in a group, both by modelling it yourself and then giving others a go.	30 minutes
Prayer: pray in response to the Bible's message, and for different aspects of the ministry.	10 minutes
People work: talk about the pastoral needs and situation of particular people in the congregation—people that the team is ministering to or could minister to. Confidentiality principles need to be agreed and respected, but talking together about how to minister to real people, and help them grow, is a powerful aspect of ministry training.	20 minutes
Prayer: pray for particular people in your congregation by name.	15 minutes
Review ministry activities: talk about different events or programs, such as last Sunday's church meeting. Did they work? Why/why not? What could be improved, and how? This not only leads to improvements, but also trains the team in how to think about ministry.	15 minutes
Training input: specific training in conviction, character and competence. This could be a session on a theological topic (e.g. the theological significance of the resurrection), or a discussion of some aspect of godly character (e.g. how we are tempted by greed), or teaching a particular ministry skill (e.g. how to lead a small group, or how to read the Bible with someone one to one).	30 minutes

With a group like this, you might set out the following expectations for the year:

- attendance at each team meeting for the year
- an hour's homework/preparation in relation to each meeting
- willingness to start meeting one to one with at least one person in the second half of the year.

You might also put a vision before each member of the group of what you hope to achieve in conviction, character and competence. For example:

- **conviction**—a deeper understanding of the cross of Christ, the Trinity, and the purpose of church
- **character**—establishing (or re-establishing) a godly discipline of prayer and Bible reading
- **competence**—training each person how to meet one to one with someone else to read the Bible.

These are just brief examples to illustrate what we hope is a self-evident principle—namely, that if we are going to call people to labour alongside us in ministry, then we need to enthuse and excite them about the magnitude of what we are doing (making disciples for Christ!), and to set clear, realistic and attainable goals and expectations for their training.

Co-workers, vine-workers and the bigger picture

Let's summarize where we've got to.

1. What is God doing in the world? God is calling people into his kingdom through Spirit-backed gospel preaching. He is growing a great worldwide vine, which is Christ and the people who are joined to him.
2. Everyone who by God's grace becomes a disciple of Christ is not only part of the vine, but also a vine-worker, a disciple-maker, a partner in the gospel. Although some Christians

have particular gifts and responsibilities for teaching and oversight, all Christians have a role in prayerfully speaking the word of truth to each other and to those outside.

3. Training is the process of growing mature Christian vine-workers—that is, Christians who are mature enough in their faith to look for opportunities to serve others by prayerfully speaking God's truth to them. This is our aim in people work. It involves not just ministry skills and competencies, but growth in convictions (understanding) and character (godliness). This is a fundamental aspect of church life, and might involve a shift in the way we think about church (especially with respect to our reliance on sermons as the only means of growth).

4. Training (understood in this way) is the engine of gospel growth. People move from being outsiders and unconverted through to being followed up as new Christians and then growing into mature, stable Christians who are then in turn trained and mobilized to lead others through the 'gospel growth' process.

5. Recruiting and training a smaller group of co-workers is the first step towards recruiting and training all Christians as vine-workers. You can't personally minister to and train 130 people. But you can start with ten, and those ten can work beside you—not only to minister personally to others, but to *train* others as well, who in turn will minister to others. The 'co-workers', in other words, are not a different category— they are just a bunch of gifted potential 'vine-workers' who work beside you to get things moving. It's ministry multiplication through personal training, and it is one of the great needs of the contemporary church.

Say we have a large number of people to be ministered to, ranging from non-Christian contacts through to new Christians and Christians in need of help. We want all of them to make progress, to grow in the gospel. We want all of them, in the end, to get to the point where they are disciple-making disciples (or 'vine-workers'). In many churches, the number of 'disciple-makers' is very small. It might just be the pastor and his assistant, plus a couple of very keen lay-people. So it might look like this:

Figure 1

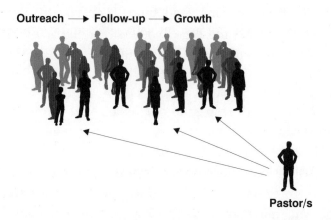

The path to growth—and not just numerical growth, but real, spiritual 'gospel' growth—is to start training people as disciple-makers; to select some of the mature Christians and excite them with the vision of disciple-making; to select what we have called in this chapter 'co-workers'. So it starts to look like this:

Figure 2

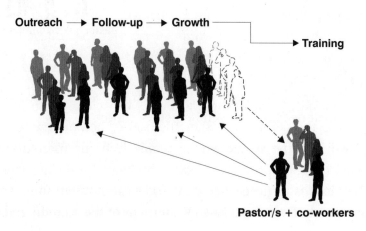

Now you as the pastor are not doing all of the ministry. You are training others to work alongside you, starting with just a few. However, the goal over time is to 'convert' all the disciples into disciple-makers, to train all the Christians as vine-workers— people with the conviction, character and competency to minister to others. So the number of workers grows, and the amount of ministry grows, as more and more people start prayerfully speaking the Bible's message to others in a myriad of different ways—large and small, formal and informal, at home, at work, at church, in small groups, and one to one.

It looks more like this:

Figure 3

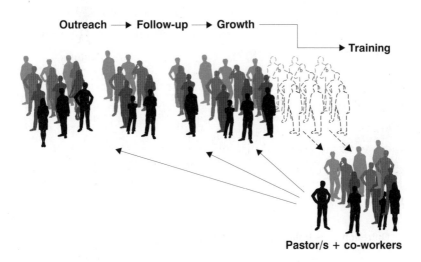

Outreach ⟶ Follow-up ⟶ Growth ⟶ Training

Pastor/s + co-workers

In other words, selecting some co-workers up-front is the first step towards creating a growing fellowship of workers of all different kinds. Some of these will work very closely with you, and get to the point where they themselves become trainers. They will not just do the work, but will lead and train other vine-workers.

We don't want to get too neat and tidy about all this—as if people start wearing badges and uniforms according to whether they are 'stable Christians', 'regular vine-workers', 'co-workers' or 'pastors'. Ministry is always messy because it involves real people. Some people you select as co-workers will end up dropping out or not realizing their potential. Others whom you didn't originally start working with will come powering through and quickly become part of the core team. Over time, the line between 'co-worker' and 'vine-worker' will become very blurred, because you will be training an ever-growing percentage of the stable Christians in your congregation to be vine-workers. And as more and more Christians are trained to minister to others, the number and variety of ministries will quickly get out of hand. People will be starting things, taking initiative, meeting with people, dreaming up new ideas. Growth is like this. It creates a kind of chaos, like a vine that constantly outgrows the trellis by sending tendrils out in all directions.

There is an aspect of this growth that we haven't yet touched upon. In Figure 3 (above), we see more and more people being ministered to because more people are being trained as vine-workers. Yet there is still only one pastor leading the whole thing and holding it together. If under God it all keeps growing, then we'll need more pastors, more overseers and more leaders.

Where are they going to come from?

Chapter 10

People worth watching

Where do pastors and other 'recognized gospel workers' come from?

The traditional answer—and it is a very good answer—is that they are called and raised up by God. Jesus asks his disciples to "pray earnestly to the Lord of the harvest to send out labourers into his harvest" (Luke 10:2). Evangelists, pastors and teachers are the gifts of the ascended Christ to his church (Eph 4:10-12).

However, to say that God provides pastors doesn't really help us all that much in knowing what part human action plays in the process. We could say, for example, that people only become Christians because God works in their hearts, but this doesn't mean that evangelism is a waste of time. On the contrary, it is precisely by means of prayerful evangelism that God graciously converts people and brings them to new birth.

God's action and human action aren't alternatives, like deciding who will perform the action of washing up tonight. God works in our world, but he isn't a creature. He's the creator, and his characteristic mode of operation is to work in and through his creatures to achieve his purposes. "I planted," says Paul, "Apollos watered, but God gave the growth" (1 Cor 3:6).

So our question would be better framed like this: By what means, or through what agency, does God call and raise up the next generation of pastors and evangelists?

We want to suggest in this chapter that it is by pastors actively recruiting suitable people within their churches, and challenging them to expend their lives for the work of the gospel. It is by doing what Paul urged Timothy to do: "...and what you have heard from me in the presence of many witnesses entrust to faithful men who will be able to teach others also" (2 Tim 2:2). Commenting on this passage, Broughton Knox says:

> It must be remembered that it is the duty of ministers in the congregation to care for the spiritual welfare of that congregation, and one of the primary areas of care is the continuance of the ministry of God's word within the congregation. Thus Paul reminded Timothy that it fell within his ministerial duty to see that the ministry of God's word was effectively continued. Just as he had the truth from Paul and his fellows, he was to hand it on to faithful men who would be able to teach others also (2 Tim 2:2)—four generations of apostolic succession in the apostolic word.[1]

In many contexts today, this task of raising up the next generation is left to 'someone else out there'. It's the denomination's job, or the seminary's. Or perhaps we leave it to God to put the idea in people's hearts without any external intervention.

Whatever the reason, most of us are reluctant to challenge people to full-time gospel work. Before we go any further, we should deal with some common questions or objections to the idea of 'ministry recruitment'.

Four common questions

Question 1: All believers are called to serve, so why should some be called into 'ministry'?

One of our real problems is the word 'call'. We are used to thinking of the 'call to ministry' as a kind of individual, mystical experience, by which people become convinced that God wants them to enter the pastorate.

However, when we turn to the New Testament, we find that the language of 'calling' is not really used this way. It is almost always used to describe how God graciously 'calls' or summons people to follow him or repent, with all the privileges and responsibilities this involves. Here is a representative selection of verses:

> And we know that for those who love God all things
> work together for good, for those who are **called**
> according to his purpose. For those whom he foreknew
> he also predestined to be conformed to the image of his
> Son, in order that he might be the firstborn among
> many brothers. And those whom he predestined he also
> **called**, and those whom he **called** he also justified, and
> those whom he justified he also glorified. (Rom 8:28-30)

> ...who saved us and **called** us to a holy calling, not
> because of our works but because of his own purpose
> and grace, which he gave us in Christ Jesus before the
> ages began... (2 Tim 1:9)

> ...having the eyes of your hearts enlightened, that you
> may know what is the hope to which he has **called** you,
> what are the riches of his glorious inheritance in the
> saints... (Eph 1:18)

> ...I press on toward the goal for the prize of the upward
> **call** of God in Christ Jesus. (Phil 3:14)

God is faithful, by whom you were **called** into the fellowship of his Son, Jesus Christ our Lord. (1 Cor 1:9)

But you are a chosen race, a royal priesthood, a holy nation, a people for his own possession, that you may proclaim the excellencies of him who **called** you out of darkness into his marvelous light. (1 Pet 2:9)

I therefore, a prisoner for the Lord, urge you to walk in a manner worthy of the **calling** to which you have been **called**... (Eph 4:1)

And let the peace of Christ rule in your hearts, to which indeed you were **called** in one body. And be thankful. (Col 3:15)

To this end we always pray for you, that our God may make you worthy of his **calling** and may fulfil every resolve for good and every work of faith by his power... (2 Thess 1:11)

The Bible doesn't speak of people being 'called' to be a doctor or a lawyer or a missionary or a pastor. God calls us to himself, to be Christian. Our 'vocation' (which comes from the Latin word 'to call') is to be Christ's disciple and to obey everything that he commanded—including the commandment to make disciples of all nations. In that sense, all Christians are 'ministers', called and commissioned by God to give up their lives to his service, to walk before him in holiness and righteousness, and to speak the truth in love whenever and however they can.

However, even though we have been emphasizing in this book the 'ministry of the many', it is not in order to sideline the 'ministry of the few' but to create the conditions under which it, too, will flourish. When we train disciples to be disciple-makers, we will also inevitably discover some godly gifted people who have the potential to be ministry leaders—to be given the privilege, responsibility and stewardship of being set apart to preach the gospel and lead God's people.

The two main categories of these 'set apart' people in the New Testament are the elders/pastors/overseers who are charged with teaching and leading congregations, and the members of Paul's apostolic gospel team, the 'fellow workers' and 'ministers', who labour for the spread of the gospel. These categories are not hard and fast, as if the pastors are not also to evangelize (cf. 2 Timothy 4:5 where Timothy is told to "do the work of an evangelist"), or as if Paul the evangelist did not also labour to build up the Christians who had been converted under his ministry. In the end, the distinction between 'evangelizing' and 'pastoring' is a blurry one.

This, in fact, is one of our problems in thinking and talking about this whole area. It all seems so blurry! And the standard Western pattern of having a professional paid pastor or clergyman doesn't always correspond. We struggle to speak in the language of the Bible not only because of the often confusing and inconsistent way that language has been used in Christian history, but also because the Bible itself does not bother to come up with precise labels. Consider these distinctions:

- All Christians should teach each other (Col 3:16), and yet not all are teachers (1 Cor 12:29; Jas 3:1).
- All Christians should 'minister' to one another (1 Pet 4:10-11), and yet some are set apart as 'ministers' (or 'deacons' or 'servants', depending on your translation, in 1 Timothy 3:8-13; see also Paul's team members, whom he calls 'ministers').
- All Christians should abound in the work of the Lord (1 Cor 15:58), and yet Paul regards himself and Apollos as 'fellow workers' labouring among the Corinthians for their growth (1 Cor 3:5-9).
- All Christians should make disciples and speak to others about Christ (Matt 28:19; 1 Pet 3:15), and yet some are identified as 'evangelists' (Eph 4:11).

There is both continuity and discontinuity. We're all in it together, and yet some have a special role. When we try to discern what it is that makes that role special in the New Testament, it's not full-time versus part-time, or paid versus unpaid. (This is a reality that pastors in the developing world understand very well.) It's not that some belong to a special priestly class and others don't. It's not even that some are gifted and others aren't, because all have gifts to contribute to the building of Christ's congregation.

The key thing seems to be that some are set apart or recognized or chosen—because of their convictions, character and competency—and *entrusted* with the responsibility under God for particular ministries. This entrusting will happen through human processes of deliberation and decision, but it remains a solemn divine trust, a stewardship of the gospel for which we are answerable to God (cf. 1 Cor 4:1-5). It is not a 'career decision' that people make casually on their own, and then equally casually decide to leave aside to move onto something else, perhaps when it gets hard or inconvenient. It's worth noting with what seriousness Paul charges Timothy to stick with his ministry in 1 Timothy 4.

Perhaps, for the sake of convenience and clarity, we should call these people 'recognized gospel workers'—not recognized because they are more spiritual or closer to God or have special powers, but recognized and chosen by other elders and leaders to fulfil a particular role of stewardship, like the captain of a team or the board of directors of a company.

This leads us to a second obvious question.

Question 2: Shouldn't we wait for people to 'feel called', rather than urging them into full-time gospel work?

It has become traditional for the personal, subjective sense of 'calling' to be the determinative factor in people offering themselves for full-time Christian ministry. Perhaps it is a longing for the dramatic personal commissioning experienced by Moses at the burning bush, or by Isaiah in the temple; or perhaps it stems from a desire to anchor our decision to pursue ministry outside ourselves in the call of God. Whatever the reason, it is common to wait for someone to say to us that they 'feel called to the ministry' or that they 'think that God is calling me to be a missionary' before we start to assess their suitability.

The Bible does not speak in these terms. Search as we may, we don't find in the Bible any example or concept of an inner call to ministry. There are some who are called directly and dramatically by God (like Moses and Isaiah), but it is not a matter of discerning an inner feeling.

Almost universally in the New Testament, the recognizing or 'setting apart' of gospel workers is done by other elders, leaders and pastors. Just as Timothy was commissioned in some way by the elders (1 Tim 4:14), so he was to entrust the gospel to other faithful leaders who could continue the work (2 Tim 2:2). Likewise Titus was given responsibility by Paul for the ministry in Crete, and he in turn was to appoint elders/overseers in every town (Titus 1:5-9).

Perhaps it is right in this sense to speak of people being 'called' by God to particular ministries or responsibilities—so long as we recognize that this 'call' is mediated through the human agency of existing recognized ministers. Luther puts it like this:

God calls in two ways, either by means or without means. Today he calls all into the ministry of the Word by a mediated call, that is, one that comes through means, namely through man. But the apostles were called immediately by Christ himself, as the prophets in the Old Testament had been called by God himself. Afterwards, the apostles called their disciples, as Paul called Timothy, Titus etc. These man called bishops as in Titus 1:5ff; and the bishops called their successors down to our time, and so on to the end of the world. This is the mediated call since it is done by man.[2]

We shouldn't sit back and wait for people to 'feel called' to gospel work, any more than we should sit back and wait for people to become disciples of Christ in the first place. We should be proactive in seeking, challenging and testing suitable people to be set apart for gospel work.

Question 3: Can't we be involved in 'gospel work' without being paid?

We have been suggesting so far that people should be chosen or commissioned as gospel workers for the preaching of the gospel and the shepherding of God's people. Traditionally, we would speak about such people being called to missionary work or to the ordained ministry, and in most Western churches these would be full-time positions paid for by the gifts of God's people.

However, the method of payment and the number of hours worked per week are not the defining factors. In the New Testament, it's hard to find many examples of 'full-time paid ministry', except perhaps Paul at some stages of his mission—as in Corinth where he started out making tents with Priscilla and Aquila, but then was "occupied with the word" when Silas and Timothy arrived (probably with a financial gift from the Macedonians; see Acts 18:1-5). Even during the three years he was in Ephesus, teaching daily in the lecture hall of Tyrannus and not ceasing "night or day to admonish everyone with tears", Paul still provided for his own needs with his own hands (Acts 20:31-34; cf. 19:9).

All the same, the Bible does affirm that those who preach the gospel should make their living from the gospel (1 Cor 9:1-12;

Gal 6:6). Even if we commence our ministry by supporting ourselves, it is right for God's people to provide for their missionaries and teachers, at least in part. Within this framework, various arrangements are possible: part-time work and ministry (like Paul's 'tent-making'); financial support from Christian friends; full-time paid ministry funded through a congregation, a denomination or a parachurch organization; and so on. Much depends on the customs and wealth of the society.

In the end, it is often a pragmatic decision. If we can minister full-time with the financial support of others, we will have more time and energy to devote ourselves to prayer and the word of God. There is a certain romance to 'tent-making' not usually shared by those who actually do it. It's frustratingly hard to juggle the demanding work of pastoring a congregation with the daily grind of secular employment. Wherever possible we should facilitate full-time ministries, if only because it will usually result in more gospel work taking place.

Broughton Knox puts it like this:

> Consideration of the character of the Christian religion shows there will always be a place for full-time ministry of the word of God. The Christian religion is a religion of faith in Christ the Lord. Faith is distinguished from superstition by being based on the truth and distinguished from rashness by being based on the knowledge of the truth. All this depends on true teaching, for we are not born with a knowledge of the truth. Moreover, Christianity is a religion of personal relationship, that of fellowship. Fellowship only comes through hearing and responding to a word spoken. God relates himself to us speaking through his word and we relate to him by responding to his word. So it is plain that a ministry which conveys and makes clear the truth about God and conveys God's word to the mind and so

to the conscience of the hearer is an essential characteristic of Christianity. If this ministry dies out then Christianity dies out.

The same conclusion may be arrived at from a slightly different approach. Jesus Christ is Lord but he can exercise no Lordship nor can obedience be the response of the Christian unless the mind of Christ is known and known relevantly to the circumstances of the Christian. This again requires a teaching ministry which understands the mind of Christ and how it applies to modern circumstance and which accompanies this teaching with exhortation and admonition, directed to the conscience of the hearer. A ministry of Christian teaching and preaching is a lifetime occupation because teaching cannot be discharged without preparation, and preparation requires time. For the Christian teacher to give himself to preparation, to the study of the word of God and its relevance, was never more needed than in the present generation.[3]

The statement that Knox makes, "If this ministry dies out then Christianity dies out", is not a piece of rhetorical overstatement. It is a simple statement of fact, arrived at by reflecting on the character of Scripture and by watching what happens in churches where this teaching ministry is lost, for one reason or another.

Question 4: Does it demean people who stay in secular work?

Here's a challenging question: does calling people to 'ministry' create two classes of Christians—the special, gifted ones who aspire to the noble calling of full-time ministry, and the rest of the plebs who are consigned to working a job in order to give money to the special ones? If someone doesn't have the gifts or opportunities to engage in 'recognized gospel work', are they condemned to a second-class existence? By giving an important place to full-time gospel work, are we saying (or implying) that everyday secular work is demeaning or unimportant?

These questions arise whenever we start challenging people to set aside secular careers and ambitions and devote themselves to gospel work. It's partly a misunderstanding about the nature of ministry and the disciple-making role of all Christians, but it's also often a misunderstanding of the nature of work in God's world. It is far beyond the scope of this chapter to sketch out a biblical theology of work, but the following bullet-point summary may be helpful.

- Working is a good and fundamental part of being human in God's world. From the very beginning, mankind was placed in the garden to work it and to keep it.
- This side of the Fall, work is cursed and frustrating (and don't we often know it!), but it remains good and worthwhile and necessary.
- Christians are strongly motivated to work, not only because of the place of work in creation, but also because work (like any other field of life) is a theatre for our service of Christ. *Whatever* you do, says Paul to the Colossians, "in word or deed, do everything in the name of the Lord Jesus, giving thanks to God the Father through him" (Col 3:17).
- At a deep level, when we work at any job, we work for Christ. As Paul goes on to say in Colossians 3, "Whatever you do, work heartily, as for the Lord and not for men, knowing that from the Lord you will receive the inheritance as your reward. You are serving the Lord Christ" (Col 3:23-24).
- As Christians, we do not work in order to gain self-fulfilment or fame or personal kudos. We work not for ourselves but for others, to serve them, to not be a burden to them, and to have something to share (Eph 4:28; 1 Tim 5:8).

- Secular work is thus very valuable, worthwhile and important. But like any good thing, it can become an idol. We can start to look to our work for our significance and value.
- We must remember that only Christ's work redeems humanity. As useful and helpful as secular work is in our world, it will not save us or build Christ's kingdom. That only happens (as we saw in chapter 3) through Spirit-backed gospel preaching.

In challenging people about gospel ministry, there are two errors we commonly fall into. One is to create two classes of Christians—those who are *really* working for the Lord and seeking to proclaim his kingdom (the 'recognized gospel workers'), and the rest. In this model, making disciples is like Formula 1 motor racing. There is really only one driver, and the rest of the people involved do their bit in the background. They might work in the pits, they might help to finance the team, or they might find sponsors and organize the logos to be painted on the cars. But the driver is the superstar and the focus, and the rest of the team members are background boys. No wonder they might feel like second-class citizens.

As we've already seen, this is not how the Bible envisages gospel work. There are not two classes of disciples—we are *all* both disciples and disciple-makers. All Christians are called to deny themselves, take up their cross, and follow Jesus to death; to give up their lives to his honour and service. It's more like a football team, where each person does all they can to advance the ball downfield. There are leaders and captains, but fundamentally and above all else, everyone is a *player*. In fact, in many teams, it's not necessarily the captain who is the best player or the most valuable contributor in any given game.

The second common error is to react to the first by dissolving the distinction between gospel work and other work.

In this way of thinking, secular work is 'baptized' as work for the kingdom of God. By being a better doctor, lawyer, businessman or software engineer (although rarely, it seems, a better garbage-collector or parking-station attendant), I am helping to 'redeem the culture' and contribute in some way to the growth of God's kingdom. In this way of thinking, we shouldn't call people out of their secular careers; we should encourage them to stay where they are for God's glory.

But this, too, is a mistake. Gospel work has a unique significance in God's plans for the world. We don't make disciples of Jesus by building better bridges, but by prayerfully bringing the word of God to people. And this is the duty, joy and privilege of *every* disciple, in whatever circumstance of life they find themselves. Secular work is valuable and good, and must not be despised or downgraded. But it is not the centre or purpose of our lives, nor the means by which God will save the world. My primary identity as a Christian is not that I am an accountant or a carpenter, but that I am a disciple-making disciple of the Lord Jesus Christ. It is really of minimal significance whether I work with my hands to earn my living as a disciple-making disciple, or others support me because of the demands of the kind of disciple-making that I do. The important thing is that we are all disciple-makers together.

People worth watching

What we are saying, in effect, is that we should be talent scouts. If the current generation of pastors and ministers is responsible for calling, choosing, and setting apart the next generation, we need to be constantly on the lookout for the sort of people with the gifts and integrity to preach the word and pastor God's people. And there is some incredible ministry talent in our churches—people with extraordinary gifts in leadership, communication and management; people with vision, energy, intelligence and an entrepreneurial spirit; people who are good with people, and who can understand and articulate ideas persuasively. If these people are also godly servants of Christ who long for his kingdom, then why not headhunt them for a life of 'recognized gospel ministry'?

We may feel a certain theological ambivalence at this point. Actively recruiting talented people sounds worldly and crass. Shouldn't we just have confidence in Christ the ascended King, that he will raise up people in his own time?

It's strange how we have recourse to the sovereignty of God or of Christ at some times and not others. We don't stop evangelizing or teaching the word just because we have confidence in the sovereign God to do his work in people's hearts. We don't stop praying just because God has his perfect purposes that cannot be thwarted. We don't stop encouraging people to serve Christ and get involved in church life even though we know that Christ is the one who will ultimately build his church. God's actions and ours aren't mutually exclusive. We speak and serve and work and pray, knowing that God will work in and through all of these things to give the growth.

It's the same with raising up the next generation. We know that the Lord of the harvest will raise up labourers, but that should not stop us praying that he would do so, and actively recruiting godly, gifted people when we notice them.

What sort of people should we be looking for? From the pastoral epistles, we learn that when selecting elders, overseers and deacons we should look for people who are:

- faithful in their understanding of and commitment to God's word
- blameless in their reputation and example of godliness
- gifted in their ability to teach others
- proven in their ability to lead and manage a family.

To this basic list we could add other qualities and characteristics that often indicate people have the gifts and potential to be gospel workers:

- communicators who speak and persuade for a living (like salesmen, teachers, real estate agents or lawyers)
- entrepreneurs who have the drive and intelligence to see possibilities and start something new
- natural leaders who influence and inspire others simply by the integrity and force of their character
- academically gifted people who could apply their intellect to theology, teaching, leadership and strategy
- people with the potential to reach particular groups in our community or overseas by virtue of their ethnicity, language ability, work background or hometown.

As we work with people in our congregations, we should be on the lookout for people with these qualities, or with the potential to develop these qualities. These are the 'people worth watching', the potential gospel workers of the next generation. If you begin to notice someone like this in your congregation, ask yourself some of the following questions:

- Is he (or she) genuinely converted and able to articulate his faith in Christ?
- Is he reading and asking questions about the Bible and theology?
- Is he faithful in applying the Bible to his thinking and life?
- Is he humble and teachable?
- Is he faithful and trustworthy?
- Is there any past or present sin that could bring Christ's name into dishonour?
- Does he serve others without being asked?
- Does he work at evangelism?
- Is he a natural communicator?

- Does he show leadership in his school, work or sporting life?
- Are others following him because of his ministry?
- Do people respond to his ministry positively?
- Is his family life healthy?
- Does he relate well to others?
- Is his spouse committed to ministry as well?
- Is he emotionally stable and tough? Will he be able to face criticism, disappointment and failure?

The kind of person who ticks these boxes has the potential to grow into a 'recognized gospel worker'. And one of the most useful stepping-stones along this path is a ministry apprenticeship.

Endnotes

1. DB Knox, *Sent by Jesus: Some aspects of Christian ministry today*, Banner of Truth, Edinburgh, 1992, p. 14.
2. Martin Luther, *Luther's Works*, American edn, vol. 26, *Lectures on Galatians*, ed. J Pelikan, Concordia, St Louis, 1963 (1535), pp. 13-78, cited in R Paul Stevens, *The Six Other Days*, Eerdmans, Grand Rapids, 2000 (1999), pp. 154-5.
3. DB Knox, *D. Broughton Knox Selected Works,* vol. 2, *Church and Ministry,* ed. Kirsten Birkett, Matthias Media, Sydney, 2003, pp. 213-214.

Chapter 11

Ministry apprenticeship

What happens between someone showing the potential to be set apart for particular responsibilities in gospel work, and them arriving at that point (as a missionary for example, or an evangelist, or a pastor in a congregation)? The normal answer is 'seminary' or 'theological college'. However, a growing number of churches and ministry candidates are making use of an intermediate step—a ministry traineeship or apprenticeship, which comes before formal theological education, and tests and trains and develops people along the path to full-time ministry.

An organization close to both of the authors' hearts—the Ministry Training Strategy (MTS)—has spent the past 20 years helping churches set up two-year ministry apprenticeships of this kind in churches throughout Australia, with offshoots in Canada, Britain, France, the Republic of Ireland, Northern Ireland, Singapore, New Zealand, Taiwan, Japan, Chile and South Africa. The basic idea is that 'people worth watching' are recruited into a two-year, full-immersion experience of working for a church or other Christian ministry. Their convictions, character and competencies are tested and developed. Under the supervision of an experienced minister, they 'catch' the nature and rhythms of Christian ministry, picking up valuable lessons and skills, and testing their suitability for long-term gospel work.

The MTS apprenticeship began in 1979 when Phillip Jensen started training a few keen, able university graduates who had a heart for God. At the time, there was no long-term vision or plan for expansion. But since 1979, over 1200 MTS apprentices have been trained in churches and campus ministries throughout Australia. Of these, over 200 are currently engaged in theological study in various colleges, and another 400 plus men and women have completed their formal studies and are now serving as full-time ministry workers worldwide.[1]

One of the most frequent questions we have been asked over the years is: *Why bother with an apprenticeship?* Given that we send our apprentices on to formal theological study, does the apprenticeship really add anything significant? It's a big sacrifice for ministry candidates to spend an extra two years training, and it's a big ask for pastors and churches to provide mentoring and remuneration for apprentices who are often raw and untested. What benefits have we seen for those who do a ministry apprenticeship? Here are a few reflections.

1. Apprentices learn to integrate word, life and ministry practice
In the classroom, imparting and processing information is the focus, and it is not always immediately obvious how the word shapes all of life and ministry. There is an inevitable and quite appropriate level of abstraction. However, in a ministry apprenticeship, the trainer and the apprentice study the Scriptures together week by week, and wrestle with their application to pastoral issues, theological fashions and ministry plans. The apprentice learns to think biblically and theologically about everything, and works this out practically with his trainer.

2. Apprentices are tested in character
A pastor working closely with an apprentice can see what might not be seen in the classroom context. The gap between

image and reality is exposed in the pressures and hassles of ministry life. The real person is revealed—the true motivations, the capacity for love and forgiveness, the scars and pain from the past, and so on. A wise trainer can build the godly character of the young minister through the word, prayer, accountability and modelling.

3. Apprentices learn that ministry is about people, not programs
We know that ministry is about the transformation of people and the building of godly communities through the gospel. More than anything else, an apprenticeship is two years of working with people—meeting with unbelievers, discipling young Christians, training youth leaders, leading small groups or comforting those who are struggling. Our goal is that apprentices spend 20 hours of their week in face-to-face ministry with people, Bible open. They learn firsthand that ministry is about people, not structures.

4. Apprentices are well-prepared for formal theological study
During the two years of ministry involvement, many biblical and theological issues are raised and discussed in the proper context of evangelism and church-building. By the end, apprentices are eager for the opportunity to pursue these questions rigorously in further study. The motivation and context for further study becomes life and ministry preparation, rather than passing exams.

5. Apprentices learn ministry in the real world
One of the problems with the classroom is that the student does not need to own the ideas in the same way as he would in the pulpit or in one-to-one pastoral ministry. His learning is abstracted from everyday life and ministry. He learns about ten different views of the atonement in order to pass his exams,

and not because anything hangs on the differences between them. Teaching the truth to others helps the apprentice understand the importance of theological training.

Another problem with a purely academic training model is that it suits certain personalities (i.e. those disposed to reading, thinking, analyzing and writing). However, some of our best evangelists and church-planters might be people who struggle in the classroom. These people thrive in a context where they are talking and preaching and building ministries while being tutored along the way. In academia they would be deemed failures.

6. Apprentices learn to be trainers of others so that ministry is multiplied

Because apprentices have had the experience of being personally mentored in life and ministry, they imbibe what we call 'the training mindset'. When they are leading a ministry in the future, they instinctively equip co-workers and build ministry teams. Those who only learn ministry in the classroom often do not catch the vision of entrusting the ministry to others. Those who were trained as apprentices tend to look for their own apprentices when they are leading a church.

7. Apprentices learn evangelism and entrepreneurial ministry

Apprenticeships provide an opportunity to think strategically and creatively about ministry. In our post-Christian, pluralistic, multicultural missionary context, many pastors no longer have a flock sitting in the pews waiting for the Sunday sermon. Apprentices can experiment with new ways of reaching people and taking the initiative to start new groups and programs.

IN MANY WAYS MTS IS AN APPLICATION OF PAUL'S WORDS TO Timothy: "...what you have heard from me in the presence of many witnesses entrust to faithful men who will be able to teach others also" (2 Tim 2:2). As Paul draws near to the end, he knows that the continued faithful proclamation of the gospel will not be secured by the writing of doctrinal confessions, or by the creation of institutional structures (as important as these are in their own way). The gospel will only be guarded and spread as it is passed from one faithful hand to the next, as each generation of faithful preachers pass their sacred trust on to the next generation, who in turn teach and train others.

MTS is really about passing on the gospel baton to the next generation of runners. The MTS handbook of ministry apprenticeship—called *Passing the Baton*—has lots of information about what two-year apprenticeships can achieve, how to set them up and run them, how to recruit and train apprentices, and so on. We won't repeat the information here.

However, it's worth thinking further about where we've come to in the cycle of training and growth. We began, you may recall, by saying that all Christians should be trained to be disciple-making disciples—trained in their knowledge of God (convictions), their godliness (character) and their ability to serve and minister to others (competencies). We suggested that the way to begin was to choose just a small number of potential co-workers and start to train them, in the expectation that some of these co-workers would in turn be able to train others. As this cycle of training continues, a workforce of disciple-makers starts to form—people who labour alongside you to help other people make progress in 'gospel growth'.

As you keep discipling and training, you begin to notice certain people with real potential for ministry—people worth watching. These are the people you challenge and recruit as the next generation of 'recognized gospel workers'. They embark on a ministry apprenticeship, and then go to Bible or theological college, after which they head off into ministry to begin training disciples... and the cycle starts again.

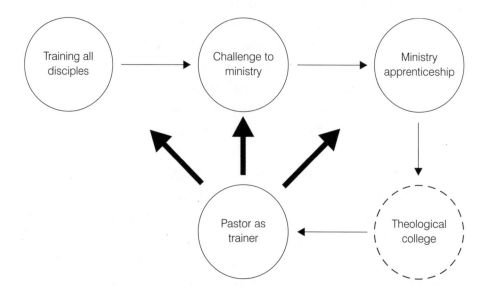

At least, that's how the theory goes. In reality, of course, it tends to be messier and less easy to chart. Some ministry apprentices don't go on to theological college—their two-year stint helps them realize (or helps their trainers realize) that they don't have either the character or the competencies for recognized gospel work. For those who do go through theological college, an enormous variety of ministry opportunities awaits them on the other side—from becoming a missionary overseas, to pastoring a congregation, to returning to secular work and being a volunteer co-worker in a new church-plant.

It also gets messy because sometimes we recruit the wrong people. There are a number of common mistakes:

- We only recruit people like ourselves—people who fit with our own particular personality or style of ministry.

- We overlook the maverick or the revolutionary, who is harder to train but might evangelize nations.
- We miss the creative or intuitive person, who is poor administratively but will reach people in ways we haven't thought of.
- We recruit the flashy, outgoing young superstar rather than the person of real character and substance.
- We recruit only for one kind of ministry—usually the traditional form of it in our denomination—rather than starting with a gifted, godly person and thinking about what kind of ministry might be built around them.
- We don't let people escape from the box into which we've put them; we don't let them outgrow the first impressions we have of them.
- We wait too long to recruit someone, and they make family or career decisions that close off ministry options.

Whoever you recruit, one hard truth must be faced: recruiting people for ministry, training them as apprentices, and sending them off to Bible college will result in a steady departure of your best and most gifted church members. This is a challenge to your gospel heart. What are you more interested in: the growth of your particular congregation, or the growth of the kingdom of God? Are you committed to church growth or to gospel growth? Do you want more numbers in the pew now, or more labourers for the harvest over the next 50 years?

It's easy to give the right answer in theory. But faith without works is dead. We demonstrate our trust in the power of the gospel, and in the worldwide kingdom of Christ, when we keep pushing our best and brightest young people out the door and off into gospel work.

The marvellous thing about generosity is that God loves it, and blesses it. In our experience, those churches that don't try to hold on to their people, but continually train them and generously export them off into further training and ministry elsewhere, are the churches that God showers with more and more new people to train.

The training mentality is an engine of growth and dynamism. It multiplies ministry because it multiplies ministers. It continually generates and develops disciple-making disciples— both within our congregations and abroad in the world—to the glory of the Lord Jesus, whose authority extends over all, even to the end of the age.

Endnote

1. See appendix 3 for a fascinating interview between Col Marshall and Phillip Jensen about MTS training.

Chapter 12

Making a start

We began, some time ago it now seems, with a vine, a trellis, and the Great Commission. And we made a promise at the start that we would offer no new special technique, no magic bullet, and no guaranteed path to ministry success and stardom.

We did this because Christian ministry is really not very complicated. It is simply the making and nurturing of genuine followers of the Lord Jesus Christ through prayerful, Spirit-backed proclamation of the word of God. It's disciple-making.

This is not hard to understand, nor even hard to do—unless, of course, you happen to be a sinful person living in a sinful world. The deceptively simple task of disciple-making is made demanding, frustrating and difficult in our world, not because it is so hard to grasp but because it is so hard to persevere in.

This is why we are such suckers for the latest ministry expert, who has always grown a church of at least 5000 from scratch, and who has a guaranteed method for growing your church to be like his. Every five or ten years, a new wave comes through. It might be the seeker-service model, or the purpose-driven model, or the missional-cultural-engagement model, or whatever the next thing will be. All of these methodologies have good things going for them, but all of them are equally beside the point—because our goal is not to grow churches, but to make disciples.

Let's tie together our thoughts with the following propositions.

1. Our goal is to make disciples

The aim of Christian ministry is not to build attendance on Sunday, bolster the membership roll, get more people into small groups, or expand the budget (as important and valuable as all of these things are!). The fundamental goal is to make disciples who make other disciples, to the glory of God. We want to see people converted from being dead in their transgressions to being alive in Christ; and, once converted, to be followed up and established as mature disciples of Jesus; and, as they become established, to be trained in knowledge, godliness and skills so that they will in turn make disciples of others.

This is the Great Commission—the making of disciples. The touchstone of a thriving church is that it is making genuine disciple-making disciples of Jesus Christ.

2. Churches tend towards institutionalism as sparks fly upward

Churches inevitably drift towards institutionalism and secularization. The focus shifts from the vine to the trellis—from seeing people grow as disciples to organizing and maintaining activities and programs. As pastors, we come to think only in structural and corporate terms. We fret about getting people into groups, increasing numbers at various programs, putting on events for people to come to, and so on. We stop thinking and praying about *people* and where each one is up to in gospel growth, and focus instead on driving a range of group activities—attendance at which (we assume) will equal growth in discipleship.

But going to groups and activities doesn't generate growth in discipleship, any more than going to hear the Sermon on the Mount made you a disciple of Jesus. Many of those who hung around with Jesus, and followed him at different times, were not genuine disciples. The crowds flocked to him for many reasons, but they just as quickly flocked away again.

3. The heart of disciple-making is prayerful teaching

The word 'disciple' means, above all else, 'learner' or 'pupil'. And this is how we become disciples and grow as disciples: by hearing and learning the word of Christ, the gospel, and having its truth applied to our hearts by the Holy Spirit. The essence of 'vine work' is the prayerful, Spirit-backed speaking of the message of the Bible by one person to another (or to more than one). Various structures, activities, events and programs can provide a context in which this prayerful speaking can take place, but without the speaking it is all trellis and no vine.

4. The goal of all ministry—not just one-to-one work—is to nurture disciples

There is no one pure context or structure for discipling. In some places, the 'discipling movement' has hijacked the language of disciple-making to imply that only one-to-one mentoring constitutes true disciple-making, and that church meetings, small groups and other corporate gatherings do not. *The goal of all Christian ministry, in all its forms, is disciple-making.* The sermon on Sunday should aim to make disciples, as should the small group that meets on Tuesday night, the men's breakfast that happens once a month, and the informal gathering of Christian friends that happens on Saturday afternoons.

The pendulum seems to swing in these matters. As we write this, in most of the churches we know and visit, the problem is that there is not nearly enough one-to-one personal work happening. Structured activities and group events have taken over, and those on the pastoral team spend their time organizing and managing rather than chasing and discipling and training people. They themselves spend very little time working with and training individuals, and those individuals in turn spend very little time meeting with and training other individuals. The focus has shifted away from individuals and their growth as disciples, to activities and events and growth in numbers.

5. To be a disciple is to be a disciple-maker

Jesus gave his disciples a vision for worldwide disciple-making. No corner of creation is off limits, and no disciple is exempt from the work.

We naturally shrink from the radical nature of this challenge. It replaces our comfortable, cosy vision of the 'nice Christian life' with a call for all Christians to devote their lives to making disciples of Jesus.

'Disciple-making' is a really useful word to summarize this radical call, because it encompasses both reaching out to non-Christians and encouraging fellow Christians to grow like Christ. As Matthew 28 says, to "make disciples" is to baptize people into Christ, teaching them to obey all that Jesus commanded. Disciple-making, then, refers to a massive range of relationships and conversations and activities—everything from preaching a sermon to teaching a Sunday school class; from chatting over the proverbial back fence with a non-Christian neighbour to writing an encouraging note to a Christian friend; from inviting a family member to hear the gospel at a church event to meeting one to one to study the Bible with a fellow Christian; from reading the Bible to your children to making a Christian comment over morning tea at the office.

6. Disciple-makers need to be trained and equipped in conviction, character and competence

If this disciple-making vision is correct, then an integral part of making disciples is teaching and training every disciple to make other disciples. This training is not simply the imparting of certain skills or techniques. It involves nurturing and teaching people in their understanding and knowledge (their convictions), in their godliness and way of life (their character), and in their abilities and practical experience of ministering to others (their competence).

This sort of training is more like parenthood than the class-room. It's relational and personal, and involves modelling and imitation. For most congregations and ministries, thinking about training in this way will require a number of significant 'mind-shifts' about ministry—from running programs and events to focusing on and training people; from using people to growing people; from maintaining structures to training new disciple-makers.

7. There is only one class of disciples, regardless of different roles or responsibilities

All Christians should be disciple-makers, and should seek to 'grow the vine' whenever and however we can. However, among the variety of gifts and roles that different Christians have in this task, some are given particular responsibility as pastors, overseers and elders to teach, to warn, to rebuke, and to encourage. These are the foremen and organizers of Christ's disciple-making vision, the guardians and mobilizers, the teachers and role models. Pastors, elders and other leaders provide the conditions under which the rest of the congregation can get on with vine work—with prayerfully speaking God's truth to others.

At a profound level, all pastors and elders are just players on the team. They do not have a different essence or status, or a fundamentally different task—as if they are the players, and the rest of the congregation are spectators or support crew. A pastor or elder is one of the vine-workers who has been given a particular responsibility to care for the people and to equip the people to be disciple-makers.

8. The Great Commission, and its disciple-making imperative, needs to drive fresh thinking about our Sunday meetings and the place of training in congregational life

What stands in the way of Christ's disciple-making vision in Christian congregations? In most cases, it's not a lack of people to train, or non-Christians to reach out to, but stifling patterns and traditions of church life. These obstacles may be denominational and long-standing; or they may be the result of jumping on board the latest church-growth bandwagon. They may be in the mind of the pastor, or the minds of the people, or—most likely—both.

If the goal of all our ministry is disciple-making, then many churches (and their pastors) will need to do some re-thinking about what they are seeking to achieve in their regular Sunday gatherings, and how that relates to other ministry activities during the rest of the week. This may mean starting new things, but very often it will mean closing down structures or programs that no longer effectively serve the goal of disciple-making. It may mean clearing out some of the regular activities and events so that congregation members actually have time to do some disciple-making—to meet with non-Christian friends, to get together one to one with newcomers at church, and so on. It may mean a revolution in the way the church staff see their ministry—not as service-providers, or managers, but as trainers.

9. Training almost always starts small and grows by multiplying workers

The temptation with training is always to start a new program— to run a multitude of training courses, and whack as many members of the congregation through them as possible. We bring our structural, event-based, managerial mindset to the task of training, and try to work out how to do it in bulk and efficiently. But you can't really train people this way any more than you can parent this way. Training is personal and relational, and it takes time. It involves sharing not just skills, but also knowledge and character. It involves imitation and modelling. Training courses and other resources are very useful tools to help us with this task. They can save enormous amounts of time (in not having to devise and refine training content ourselves), and can provide excellent frameworks within which the personal, relational work of training can take place. But it must start with people, and focus on people—not programs.

In other words, if we want to start training disciples to be disciple-makers, we need to build a network of personal ministry in which people train people. And this can only begin if we choose a bunch of likely candidates and begin to train them as co-workers. This group will work alongside you, and in time will themselves become trainers of other co-workers. Some of your co-workers will fulfil their potential and become fruitful fellow labourers and disciple-makers. Others will not. But there is no avoiding this. Building a ministry based on people rather than programs is inevitably time-consuming and messy.

10. We need to challenge and recruit the next generation of pastors, teachers and evangelists

When the training engine begins to gather steam, and people within your congregation are being mobilized into ministering to others, some 'people worth watching' (PWWs) will float to the surface—people strong in conviction, character and competence. These PWWs are the potential 'recognized gospel workers' of the next generation. And if you are a pastor or elder, it is one of your God-given responsibilities to recognize, nurture, train and entrust the gospel to these "faithful men who will be able to teach others" (2 Tim 2:2).

Many churches have found a ministry apprenticeship program to be an extremely effective way of advancing this process (such as the one developed and supported by the Ministry Training Strategy).

Making a start

We hope that reading this book has set your mind racing with ideas and challenges for the ministry you are engaged in. However, it is often difficult to translate a racing mind into a set of concrete goals or action steps.

To help your thinking and planning, here is *just one* suggested plan for starting to reshape your ministry around people and training, rather than around programs and events.

Step 1: Set the agenda on Sundays

If you want to change the culture of your congregation in the direction of disciple-making and training, then this new direction needs to shape your regular Sunday gatherings.

You could, for example, preach a sermon series on 'What is gospel growth?', or on 'Disciples and disciple-making'. You could set out the biblical vision of the Great Commission, and how it leads to disciples who make other disciples.

But more than that, in your regular exposition of the Scriptures:

- show how the gospel of grace shapes a life of praise and sacrifice for Christ
- enthuse the congregation with the grand eternal purposes of God to make disciples and build a fellowship of disciples under Christ's lordship
- call the congregation to radical discipleship
- communicate the expectation that what is being taught from the pulpit is what also should be passed on to others (you might provide summaries or discussion questions for use in personal ministry)

- preach in a way that helps the congregation learn to read and speak about the Bible themselves; show how you arrived at your conclusions from the text
- tackle apologetic and pastoral issues that will be useful not only to those present, but also to others via the personal ministry of those present.

It's not only the sermon that sets the agenda and starts to change congregational culture. In your church meetings, get members up the front to share about ministries they are involved in. Don't just get the superstars or the success stories; provide examples for the congregation of people who are stepping out of their comfort zones and trying something new.

This also flows into what we pray for in our gatherings. Make the various personal ministries of congregation members a regular subject for corporate prayer.

We can also build a culture of training into the way people contribute to the gathering. Provide training and feedback for those who are participating—in music, Bible reading, praying, sharing a testimony, welcoming newcomers, and so on.

Step 2: Work closely with your elders or parish council

In building a disciple-making and training emphasis in your congregation, it's obviously vital that the existing elders and leaders of the congregation are fully included in the thinking, planning and decision-making. Here's an example of how one pastor went about it:

> When introducing the Ministry Training Strategy into the Christian Reformed Churches of Australia (CRCA), we had to bear in mind that these churches are governed by a system of elders in each congregation. All decisions about the life and direction of the church are made by the elders that form the church council.

So when Colin Marshall invited me to join his Art of Ministry Training course [a forerunner of this book], I knew that I had to get my eldership team on board as well. I asked Colin for permission to photocopy the reading assignments for my elders. It became required reading before each church council meeting, and then we discussed the readings for the first half-hour. I did this throughout that year, so that by the time I finished the course, the elders had also done the readings.

Having completed the course, and being very keen to get into it, I asked the elders what they thought. They agreed it would be part of what we do as a church. What was important about how we processed it was that they were on the journey with me. They had time to assimilate all the new ideas. They had time to reflect and make it their own, so that when I asked them at the end of that year, "Shall we do it?", they were ready to go.

It is so important to give your leaders the time to process stuff and come to terms with it and own it. I say this because my colleagues did not take the steps I took, and when they put it to their local church councils many found resistance to these 'new ideas'. Several colleagues asked me to address their elders and I spent an evening in those churches workshopping the main concepts of ministry training. It was delightful to see the 'light go on' for some of the senior elders, who went on to encourage their minister to set up training in their church.

In the CRCA this processing by the elders needs to be an ongoing thing, as our elders each serve for a term of three years. I train all my new elders for six months. This training process, and the four workshops we run on what MTS is and how it works, has them keen about the training mindset by the time they are inducted as leaders of the church. Seeing young men coached in preaching, Bible study leaders trained, and an apprentice learning the skills of ministry has given the elders the sense that we are a training church; it is part of our DNA now. It's all about developing a mindset: 'this is how we do church'. It's being faithful to 'making disciples' and 'equipping the saints for ministry'. It's what we need to do if we want pastors, evangelists and church leaders now and for the future.

Building some form of regular training and 'ministry talk' into the agenda of church council meetings is very useful. Over time, it cements the eldership team together as co-workers in the gospel, rather than as a council of regulators and accountants. Decisions are made through the prism of gospel growth.

Over time, we can also create the expectation that being an elder or parish councillor also means being engaged in some personal ministry of the word—visiting newcomers, or meeting one to one with others, or mentoring people with potential to be leaders in the future. The overall goal is to increase unity around the common task of gospel work.

Step 3: Start building a *new* team of co-workers

The principle is: do a deep work in the lives of a few.

This is your band of brothers and sisters who would die together for the sake of the gospel; those with whom you will share your life and ministry in the expectation that they will learn to evangelize, teach and train others.

Notice that it is a *new* team. Don't just think about those who are already serving in ministries or on committees. Choose a mixture of current and future leaders that you would like to build the ministry around for the next five years.

Remember: you are not grooming people to fill gaps in your church program, but training co-workers around whom you will build ministry according to their particular gifts and opportunities. Some of these people will start new ventures in outreach or Christian growth—things you or they haven't yet imagined or thought possible.

Training this team of co-workers can be done through one-to-one meetings, group meetings, or more often a mixture of both, and includes our now familiar mix of the three C's (conviction, character and competence). See chapter 9 for more ideas about how to train a team of co-workers.

Step 4: Work out with your co-workers how disciple-making is going to grow in your context

So you are training a team of co-workers—but how is disciple-making going to grow from this base? How does it multiply? There is of course no single correct answer, because it depends so much on the gifts and circumstances of your co-workers, and the church or ministry context in which you're working. Here is just one idea to get your juices flowing.

Your congregation may already have an existing Bible study group network that is functioning reasonably well, but the real challenge you have is in helping new people (whether Christian or non-Christian) to find their way into the congregational life and be discipled. So you work with your co-workers on a visiting and follow-up ministry aimed especially at newcomers. The aim is that every newcomer or visitor to the church is personally visited in their homes, and then followed up over the next several months, until such time as they are safely and happily involved in a small group (where the group leader takes responsibility for discipling them). Your co-workers are the front-line in getting this integration process happening. You take them with you to visit newcomers, and train them in how to assess where someone is up to in 'gospel growth'. Each co-worker might personally take on two or three newcomers over a three-month period: to meet with each one several times, to evangelize them if they are not Christian, to read the Bible and pray with them, to explain the church's vision and how to become involved, to have them for lunch and introduce them to other congregation members, to call them when they don't come to church to see how they're going, and to see them join a small group.

A wealth of resources are available to assist your co-workers in meeting with newcomers to minister to them one to one. There are Bible study tools for working through the gospel with someone, or for establishing someone in the basics of Christian faith and life, or for simply reading the Bible one to one with another person. There are also excellent resources for helping you to train co-workers in these ministry skills. (See appendix 2 for examples of these resources.)

Now, this idea will only work long term if the small groups are functioning well—and, in particular, if the group leaders have been trained to see themselves not merely as facilitators or organizers but also as front-line disciple-makers and 'mini-pastors' of the people in their group. Spending regular time with your group leaders to train them in this may be your next priority!

Step 5: Run some training programs

Although we have been emphasizing the need for training to be personal—as opposed to just running people through a three-week course—there are still lots of advantages in running structured or off-the-shelf training programs. They not only provide a level of formal structure that can improve the quality of the training, but they can also function as a first step in identifying people who are suitable for more responsibility and more intensive personal training.

For example, you could encourage all your small groups to do a training course on personal evangelism in their normal group time—such as *Six Steps to Talking about Jesus* or *Two Ways to Live: Know and share the gospel*. This will give all the group members, no matter where they are up to or what their level of gift is, a basic degree of skill and confidence in being able to talk about their faith. This is something every disciple should have! However, running a course like this will usually reveal people who are really good at evangelism, and who are ripe for further training and ministry in that area.

Again, see appendix 2 for a range of high-quality programs.

Step 6: Keep an eye out for 'people worth watching'

As the number of people in training and ministry grows, keep an eye out for those with real potential. Invite one or two of them into a two-year ministry apprenticeship. (See *Passing the Baton* for all the details on how to set up and run a ministry apprenticeship.)

The long-term goal might be to see these apprentices do some further formal training, and then return to the congregation to work alongside you, or plant a new congregation with your support. Ministry of the kind we are talking about always generates more ministry. As more and more people are trained as disciple-makers, more and more people are contacted, evangelized and/or followed up. The amount of people work gradually mushrooms. And the need for pastors, leaders, overseers and elders grows accordingly. The number of paid staff in your congregation will thus need to grow, simply to cope with the growing number of people to be led and pastored.

PLEASE REMEMBER: THIS IS JUST ONE SET OF IDEAS ABOUT HOW to make a start. Your ministry and context will generate its own variations and challenges.

As you begin to introduce these concepts to your

congregation, be careful to keep preaching the gospel of free forgiveness through Jesus, and the life of joyful obedience that flows from it. Keep holding high the death and resurrection of Christ, and keep praying for your people. The motivation to serve and to be trained will come from the gospel and from a deep work of the Spirit in people's hearts. It won't come from you going on and on about training, and harassing people until they finally sign up! It's grace, not guilt. Don't make 'training' the new test of true discipleship.

However, the possibilities for training and growth in most congregations are endless, and endlessly exciting. And you will need to think through for yourself the possibly radical changes that need to happen. To help you do so, and as a useful way to conclude, let's try a little mental experiment.

Imagine this...

As we write, the first worrying signs of a swine-flu pandemic are making headlines around the world. Imagine that the pandemic swept through your part of the world, and that all public assemblies of more than three people were banned by the government for reasons of public health and safety. And let's say that due to some catastrophic combination of local circumstances, this ban had to remain in place for 18 months.

How would your congregation of 120 members continue to function—with no regular church gatherings of any kind, and no home groups (except for groups of three)?

If you were the pastor, what would you do?

I guess you could send regular letters and emails to your people. You could make phone calls, and maybe even do a podcast. But how would the regular work of teaching and preaching and pastoring take place? How would the congregation be encouraged to persevere in love and good deeds, especially in such trying circumstances? And what about evangelism? How would new people be reached, contacted and followed up? There could be no men's breakfasts, no coffee mornings, no evangelistic courses or outreach meetings. Nothing.

You could, of course, revert to the ancient practice of visiting your congregation house-to-house, and door-knocking in the local area to contact new people. But how as a pastor could you possibly meet with and teach all 120 adults in your congregation, let alone their children? Let alone door-knock the suburb? Let alone follow up the contacts that you made?

No, if it was to be done, you would need help. You would need to start with ten of your most mature Christian men, and meet intensively with them two at a time for the first two months (while keeping in touch with everyone else by phone and email). You would train these ten in how to read the Bible and pray with one or two other people, and with their children. Their job would then be twofold: to 'pastor' their wives and families through regular Bible reading and prayer; and to each meet with four other men to train and encourage them to do the same. Assuming that 80% of your congregation was married, then through these first ten men and those that they subsequently trained, most of the married adults would be involved in regular Bible-based encouragement.

While that was getting going (with you offering phone and email support along the way), you might choose another bunch to train personally—people who could meet with singles, or people who had potential in door-knocking and evangelism, or people who would be good at following up new contacts.

It would be a lot of personal contact, and a lot of one-to-one meetings to fit in. But remember, there would be no services to run, no committees, no parish council, no seminars, no home groups, no working bees—in fact, no group activities or events of any kind to organize, administer, drum up support for, or attend. Just personal teaching and discipling, and training your people in turn to be disciple-makers.

Here's the interesting question: after 18 months, when the ban was lifted and you were able to recommence Sunday gatherings and all the rest of the meetings and activities of church life, what would you do differently?

Appendix 1

Frequently asked questions

As we've shared these ideas with many people over the years, numerous questions have come up. Here are some of the most common.

Q1. You say that every Christian is called to be a 'vine-worker' and a 'disciple-making disciple'. I am not very good at teaching or speaking, and I don't feel that I know very much about the Bible. How can I live out the calling you are talking about?
Perhaps the best way to answer this is to pass on a conversation I had recently with some Christian friends who were in sales— one sold real estate and the other sold software.

I started to tell my friends that I sometimes find it difficult to talk easily about Christian things, especially with non-Christians, because I don't have a natural 'salesman' sort of personality—not like they do. But one of my friends pulled me up short.

"No, you don't understand sales", he said. "It's not about having a particular personality or having the gift of the gab. I've got all these guys working for me who think they're great sales-men, because they're fast-talking, ambitious 'sales' guys. But they're actually not the best salesmen. The girl who's bringing in the most business is much more laid back, but she's genuine. She communicates real concern and sincerity. She gets next to people, understands and listens to them, and then works really hard to help them get what they want. She's bringing in the business, but if you asked her, she wouldn't say she was a natural salesperson."

"It's really about whether you love the product, and know it well, and whether you actually care for people and want to see them satisfied. If you really believe in it, then you'll sell it."

My other friend the salesman chimed in at this point as well.

"Yes, that's right. You can have someone who knows the technical details of the product perfectly, but who has no passion for it, and no empathy or ability to relate to people, to listen to them. Selling is just as much about listening as anything else."

The lesson here is that although we all have different gifts and abilities, the most important factor is how much we love the message of God, and how much we love the people all around us who need to hear it. You may not be the person who is going to preach to crowds, or lead Bible study groups, but if you really long to see other people become disciples of Jesus, then you will find ways of doing that within the gifts God has given you—like Dave, the young man with schizophrenia that we mentioned in chapter 2.

Q2: I'm a pastor, and I'm convinced by your argument that in the long term, training people will not only build the ministry but also help with my time. But I barely have time to get things done now! How do I start making a start?

The first thing to say is that 'training' really is a mind-shift and not simply a new set of responsibilities or tasks. Training is mostly relational and done on-the-job. It's the kind of thing that can permeate all the different aspects of your ministry, rather than being an extra program added onto your schedule.

So when you go to visit a newcomer or a member of your congregation, take someone with you. When you're preparing your sermons, spend part of the time talking over the issues with a co-worker (it will help you and them!). As much as possible, include others in what you are doing and train them as you go. Let them see you in action; how you're thinking and reacting; how you're bringing the Bible to bear on the task at hand.

Secondly, make an honest and thorough audit of how you spend your time. What are the activities, programs and priorities that prevent you from devoting some time specifically to training? Are there good reasons for these things to be of a higher priority than training? Or do the reasons stem from unhelpful motivations—for example, a desire to meet the expectations of members, performance anxiety about preaching (leading to excessive preparation), fear of missing deadlines, personal insecurity, and so on?

Thirdly, take the long view. It may feel like there is no time for training now because of your high workload, but failing to train will only lock you permanently into this high workload trap. You feel like there's too much to do and no time for training, and so you don't train. But this means that you don't raise up helpers and co-workers who can labour alongside you in the ministry. And so you continue to bear the workload and stress alone, which over time wears you down. You end up falling victim to short-term, reactive planning and living.

Fourthly, steel yourself to say 'No', and to be disliked as a result. In most situations, saying 'Yes' to more training will inevitably mean saying 'No' to something else. And as a natural consequence you will be resisted and disliked by some of your own people, or by denominational officials, or both. Some people may even leave your church. This is hard, but unavoidable. Not everyone will share the priorities of the gospel. However, it certainly helps in this regard if you develop a set of priorities and make them public, and if you work hard at taking your elders or parish council with you (see step 2 of

'Making a start' in chapter 12).

It probably doesn't need to be said, but being disliked, and even having people leave, is not something to aim at for its own sake! We should always be checking our motivations, actions, presentations and priorities when such things happen. But sometimes we need to allow these things to happen in order for right priorities to flourish. When right priorities are kept—when you say 'No' to some people and some things—people will not like you.

Q3: I already have leaders in place. Should I still consider employing the pastor-as-trainer model?

A number of pastors I chat with assume that training is happening because they run certain programs or have small groups in place. Of course, to a degree this may very well be true. However, it is well worth evaluating your current practices with some diagnostic questions like these:

- Is there a culture of one-to-one disciple-making in your congregation?
- Do the Bible study leaders at your church know what it means to shepherd and lead the people in their groups?
- Are your leaders themselves 'training-oriented'—that is, are they seeking to raise up and train more leaders themselves?
- Does everyone in your church know a basic way to share the truth of Christianity?
- Do all of your people know how to encourage someone, with and through the word of God?
- Do all the people at your church understand what it means to serve Jesus and act out their Christian faith in everyday life?
- Do you have a group of people at your church who can teach a Bible study and get the point of the text across?

- Is there a core group of people who understand the priorities of the church and can effectively train others in those priorities?
- Are you identifying, recruiting and training those with gifts for evangelism ('lay missionaries'), and releasing them into your local community with the gospel?
- Is the next generation of gospel workers being raised up? Are you seeing new 'ministry talent' emerge?

Q4: How can I communicate a captivating vision for ministry training?

Giving people a short summary of what you—as a church or leader—are on about is important. As we've said throughout the book, we want all people to be disciple-making disciples of Christ. You will need to express this in your own way and in terms that work within your context, but it's worth putting in the work with your key leaders to craft a statement that focuses your goals. Perhaps after you have worked closely with your elders or parish council for a year or so, you could set yourself the joint task of re-casting the vision or mission of the congregation in a way that signals a shift in emphasis.

Matthias Media, for example, has recently rewritten its mission statement like this:

> We want to persuade all Christians of the truth of
> God's purposes in Jesus Christ as revealed in the
> Bible, and equip them with high-quality resources, so
> that by the work of the Holy Spirit they will:
>
> - abandon their lives to the honour and service of Christ in daily holiness and decision-making
> - pray constantly in Christ's name for the fruitfulness and growth of his gospel

- speak the Bible's life-changing word whenever and
  however they can—in the home, in the world and in
  the fellowship of his people.

How would you adapt a statement like this to express your
ministry goals?

Q5: Why won't people commit?

Lack of commitment from church members is probably the
most common reason pastors and leaders give for the lack of
training at their church.

Now, there isn't a simple cure-all solution to this one. It's
fundamentally a spiritual disease, but there are numerous
cultural, theological and historical factors that contribute to its
spread and virulence:

- **Professionalism of the ministry:** in many churches, the
  average Christian thinks that ministry is a profession,
  and since it is not *their* profession, it is not their role as a
  Christian. Pastors may bemoan this, but they should also
  take a close look in the mirror on this issue. In many
  churches, the ministry is completely controlled and
  centralized among the pastors and/or elders, in part
  because they like it that way. They have control. Things
  are orderly and predictable. Mobilizing and releasing the
  congregation for ministry is exciting, but it will also
  inevitably increase messiness and chaos.
- **A clericalized view of ministry:** this is emphasized in
  some denominations more than others but is pervasive in
  them all. Ordination is a special anointing on a special
  person for special work, so the laity are inclined to just let
  the ordained staff get on and do the ministry.
- **Niche ministry:** in his book *The Deliberate Church*, Mark
  Dever argues against specialized ministry positions

because they take the ownership of those ministries away from the congregation.[1] If there is a youth minister, then the ownership of youth ministry is not with the parents of the youth (as it should be) but with the youth minister. The structure acts as a disincentive for people to get involved.

- **Spiritual immaturity:** wanting to serve others, and to grow in that, is a function of Christian maturity. The more we become like Jesus, the more we will want to pour out our lives in love and service of others. If people in your congregation do not *want* to serve, then how effectively are they being taught and discipled? How effectively and clearly is the gospel itself being preached? Do your people know that laying down their lives for others is an integral part of being Christian? It may be time to go back to the foundations and challenge the strength of people's commitment to Jesus as their Lord. It may be time to pray that God would do a deep work in people's lives by his Spirit so that they would want to live sacrificially.

- **Not spending time with the right people:** we tend to be all-inclusive in our attempts at training and discipleship. Further, we tend to spend a great deal of our time with those in need—such as newcomers or the sick and suffering. These people are all important, but they are not the ideal people to really invest in at the outset. Instead, pick some people—or even just one person—who have a heart for growth, and start there.

- **The right people in the wrong places:** are the kinds of people you would like to start training and working with already up to their ears in committee work and other 'trellis' activities? You will need to get them out of these structures—or dismantle the structures!—if they are going to have the time and energy to devote to training.

- **Spiritual gifts:** people tend to do only what they think they are gifted at. 'Spiritual gifts inventories' were all the rage in churches in the 1990s. But getting everyone through an inventory class hasn't really helped with the 80/20 problem (80% of the work done by 20% of the people). Why not? Because the root issue is not people's lack of understanding about what their spiritual gifts are, but their motivation and understanding of ministry.

The other thing we can do to motivate participation in training is to work with live ammunition. That is, rather than simply saying, "Who'd like to come and do some training in children's ministry?", you cast a vision for a new kids' club or a ministry in the local schools. And when people are grabbed by the possibilities of this new ministry, and want to be involved, and start to be involved, they will be desperate for training. If they have to front up before a bunch of 13-year-olds every week to teach the Bible, then they will be very keen to be helped, trained, equipped and mentored in whatever way possible!

Leadership, after all, is vision—not coercion.

Q6. In your 'Making a start' section, I'm struggling to get past step 3—that is, I have a few people I could possibly start to train as co-workers, but how do I persuade them of the importance of getting involved? How do I fire them up with the desire to be trained and to minister to others?

How does this kind of personal transformation take place, such that people's hearts burn within them to want to serve Christ and other people? How can people be transformed from a worldly-minded, self-centred way of living (even as Christians) to a heavenly-minded, other-person-centred way of serving?

It can only be through the miraculous work of God in their lives, as he applies his word to their hearts by his Spirit. How do we participate in God's work?

- We pray earnestly and often for our people—that God would melt their hearts.
- We teach and apply God's word to them—from the pulpit, in smaller groups and one to one. One way to do this would be to take the material from the opening chapters of this book—especially chapters 1-6—and work through it with a key bunch of people. You might just steal the ideas and turn it into Bible studies or sermons (we don't mind!). Or you might actually work through the book one chapter at a time, with discussion and Bible study.
- We give people a taste for serving others by taking them with us as we do different things in ministry. Take someone visiting or door-knocking with you, or let them sit in as you do a Bible study with a new Christian.
- We patiently persevere. All this often takes time, depending on how mature and godly your people already are.

Q7. Why is 'training' needed alongside faithful preaching and pastoral ministry?

There is a very right instinct that says that if we prayerfully and faithfully preach the word, then people's hearts will be changed and they will want to give themselves to disciple-making and the service of others. So why do we need this separate thing called 'training'?

The answer is that 'training'—as we have defined it—is not really a separate thing, but simply the outworking of prayerful proclamation as it connects with individual people. Training is *not* just about imparting certain skills. It's a ministry of the word leading to growth in conviction, character and competence. The real power of training is not in the method or the strategy, but in the way God's word and Spirit work in people's lives.

Another way of putting it is that 'training' is the exercise of pastoral ministry before the crisis. It's how you work with each one of your people for their growth and maturity when you aren't nurturing and caring for them in their grief, sickness and family problems.

The 'training' mind-shift also adds a dimension to how well people hear and learn from your teaching. If the constant culture of your church is that every Christian is not just a hearer but also a speaker, then it changes the way they listen. There's nothing like having to explain the gospel to motivate you to actually learn what the gospel is.

Q8. What about the importance of Christian community? Is all this 'training' talk individualistic?

If the goal is to train disciple-making disciples of Jesus, then the goal is to train people who love one another as Christ our Lord commanded. In our experience, churches that have a strong culture of training (as we've defined it) end up building deep, honest, loving communities of Christ. The people in these communities no longer see themselves as consumers or spectators, but as servants wanting to see others grow.

Training may start small. It may focus on individual people, and on what each person needs in order to grow, but the result is an outbreak of love.

What also tends to happen is that as people 'get' the vision of ministry and training, and start reaching out and developing new ministries around their particular gifts and circumstances, new little fellowships of God's people develop, either as sub-groups within congregations, or as new church-plants.

Q9. How do small groups fit into your concept of training?

In many places today, a small-group network is one of the key 'trellises' of church life—a structure that allows Christians to get together to encourage each other over the Bible, and to pray for each other.

However, some pastors are rightly sceptical about the value of small groups. If small groups are not led and run well, they can easily become ineffective or even dangerous structures where people gather to share their ignorance, and where there is no genuine pastoral oversight.

Without training, delegation of pastoral ministry and responsibility to a small-group structure is an abdication of pastoral stewardship. Small groups can be very effective vehicles for ministry, but only if we train leaders to have a sound grasp of doctrine, a godly character, and the ability to understand and teach the Bible through group discussion.

Because many churches do not adequately train their people, and thus do not grow the kind of vine-workers who can lead effective small groups, leadership and teaching tends to be centralized around the ordained pastor/s and perhaps a few key lay elders. This guards the gospel, but it doesn't multiply the ministry.

Small groups can be a very useful structure *in which* to train people. If the group leader sees himself or herself not as a facilitator or chairperson but as a *trainer*, it completely changes the goals and dynamics of the group. The group leader's goal becomes the same as the goal for all ministry—not just to make disciples, but to make disciple-making disciples.

Q10. How does your approach to ministry and growth fit in with church-planting? Isn't the planting of new congregations a key strategy in the growth of the gospel?

In many respects, the 'trellis and vine' metaphor helps us to understand and clarify what's so useful and important about church-planting. It also alerts us to some dangers.

Metaphorically, we might say that if we have a trellis with a flourishing vine on one side of our yard, and we'd like to see it grow on the other side of the yard, we could take two approaches.

We could water and prune and work on the vine, while also maintaining and expanding the trellis, so that eventually the vine grows all the way across the back fence to the other side of the yard. A mega-vine, you might say. Or we could construct a new trellis on the other side of the yard, take a cutting from the original vine, and start again.

Both approaches are legitimate, and the choice between them will depend on numerous factors (not least the skill of the leadership to be able to grow and hold together a large congregation). However, many churches have found that planting new congregations in new contexts, locations and times, or with new emphases and styles, has really helped with vine growth. Growing a 'vine' from 30 or 40 members to 120 is often easier, especially in terms of the trellis complications, than growing from 120 to 200.

But here's the thing. Planting a new trellis and vine some-where won't facilitate growth if the vine is not healthy to begin with. The mere act of transplantation won't create gospel growth—that is, the evangelizing, converting and growing of disciple-making disciples of Jesus Christ. But if that sort of gospel growth *is* happening, and you plant some of those people somewhere else, the chances are that they will grow and multiply there as well with renewed enthusiasm.

In other words, the excitement over church-planting can sometimes lead people to think that the mere fact of putting up a new trellis somewhere will result in a new, healthy, growing vine. But the key thing about the church-plant is not the quality or location of the trellis, but the quality of the people—the vine-workers—who are starting the new work. Once again, it comes back to how well we are training our people to be disciple-makers.

For many, the activity of church-planting implies erecting a trellis with familiar, recognizable features: a building, an ordained minister, a constitution, and so on. But if we understand that vine work is the key thing, then we can be flexible about the particular kind of trellis needed to plant a new vine in this new location. For example, we may start with a group of Christians meeting in a lounge room without an ordained minister.

Whatever approach we take, training vine-workers is critical. We need to build teams of disciples engaged in Spirit-backed word ministry. We need to build it around the people, not the structures.

Q11. Is your approach to ministry anti-big-church? Are you saying that the 'ideal' church is a pastor-trainer with 120 people?

Absolutely not. The principles of ministry we are outlining are (we argue) the Bible's principles for making disciples of all nations. They apply as much to the small Bible study group of eight people as they do to the mega-church of 2000. That is, the goal of all ministry is to see people become godly, mature disciples of Christ, who in imitation of their Lord are longing to reach and serve others and make disciples of them as well. Training disciples in conviction, character and competence should be at the heart of all Christian ministry, regardless of the size of the fellowship and its structures.

For example, we know of a pastor who is currently grappling with how to grow his congregation from 500 to 1000. He faces organizational and structural challenges ('trellis' challenges), and the leadership and human management skills he will require are more significant than if he was pastoring a church of 80. He knows that he needs to do some work 'on the business' and not just 'in the business'. However, this particular pastor also knows that his goal is not simply to get an additional 500 people to sit in his building (which he could achieve in various ways!), but to grow 500 more disciples of Jesus. And he knows that he won't be able to find and gather and teach these new disciples on his own. It will only happen (under God) if he keeps training his people to work alongside him in outreach, follow-up, growth and training. In other words, growing a big congregation not only requires highly able and skilled leadership, but also an unwavering commitment to training an army of co-workers. It requires an even greater commitment to keeping people at the centre rather than programs.

It must be acknowledged that not everyone has the leadership abilities and personality to build and lead a large congregation. But our philosophy of ministry should lead us to support, encourage and champion those who do. Ministry should be built around people and their gifts. If someone has the gifts to build a really large and significant gospel work, let's give them every assistance and training to do it.

One other important point on this: one of our MTS trainers chose to train and send over 30 of his best leaders into gospel ministry around the world, with the result that he has not built a mega-church. These 30 leaders are now serving as pastors, church-planters, missionaries and theological educators. If he had kept them all on his staff, who knows how big his church might be today? But by intentionally and generously giving them away, the gospel has advanced on many fronts. It's a strategic choice between growing our own churches and growing the gospel beyond our local work. Of course it is possible to do both. But we must not value big churches as the only measure of gospel progress.

Q12. I am a pastor. Much of what I do is to care for those who are hurting and sick and in need. From what you are saying in chapters 8 and 9, are you really suggesting I don't do that any more?

Of course not. The sick and suffering in our congregations certainly need to be cared for. What we're suggesting is that they aren't the only ones that need your time and ministry. If you really want to care for them *and* see real gospel growth, then the wise thing to do is to train and mobilize the godly mature Christians in the congregation to do some of that caring work.

This may present some tricky choices for the pastor. We need to pray for godly wisdom. And there will be crises and needs that simply need the pastor's attention. But your responsibility as the pastor is to 'feed the sheep'—all of them. If all your time and energy is absorbed by the sick and ailing sheep, then not only will the healthier ones not be fed, but they might also end up wandering off somewhere else!

Q13. If we are encouraging people to start their own ministries, using their gifts and opportunities, won't the whole thing become a bit messy and chaotic?
Yes. And your problem with that is...?

The fact is that many of us are 'control freaks', and place too much value on having everything neat and tidy and under control. A bit of messiness is inevitable in people ministry.

However, the kind of control that is needed is the control of sound doctrine and godly character. Some administrative or organizational chaos can be managed, but the chaos of sin or false teaching does real damage. This is why it is so important to train people in conviction, character and competence so that the ministries they are involved in are godly and Bible-based.

Endnote
1. M Dever, *The Deliberate Church*, Crossway Books, 2005, pp. 161-70.

Resources for training from MTS and Matthias Media

T he philosophy of ministry in *The Trellis and the Vine* has been brewing and developing in our minds and lives over the past 30 years or so. It has spawned two 'sister' organizations:

- The Ministry Training Strategy (MTS), developed by Phillip Jensen and Colin Marshall throughout the 1980s and launched as an independent training agency in 1992
- Matthias Media, launched by Tony Payne in 1988.

Both organizations have this book in their veins (if books can be in veins), and in various ways seek to promote this ministry philosophy and provide resources to support it.

Training and apprenticeship resources from MTS

The particular focus of MTS is ministry apprenticeship. The MTS vision is to raise up 10,000 new 'gospel workers' by training trainers who, in turn, train their people and recruit the next generation.

- MTS is training ministers of the gospel to declare the saving work of Christ to the world. Our focus is to train men and women as faithful and competent Bible teachers who will serve Christ as pastors, evangelists and church-planters.

- MTS offers a two-year 'hands-on' apprenticeship program conducted in churches and specialist ministry teams. It involves on-the-job ministry training based on prayer, Bible study and practical ministry.
- MTS is identifying those who have gifts for full-time Christian ministry. We are training innovative leaders who can break new ground for the gospel. We are equipping leaders who will train others for the work of the gospel.
- MTS training is conducted around the world in churches from various denominations and in a range of evangelistic ministries.

To find out more about MTS, and to gain access to the resources and services that MTS offers, please visit our website: **www.mts.com.au**

To find out more in particular about ministry apprenticeship, read *Passing the Baton: A handbook for ministry apprenticeship* by Colin Marshall (published by Matthias Media).

Gospel growth resources from Matthias Media

Matthias Media explains its mission like this:

We want to persuade all Christians of the truth of God's purposes in Jesus Christ as revealed in the Bible, and equip them with high-quality resources, so that by the work of the Holy Spirit they will:

- abandon their lives to the honour and service of Christ in daily holiness and decision-making
- pray constantly in Christ's name for the fruitfulness and growth of his gospel

- speak the Bible's life-changing word whenever and however they can—in the home, in the world and in the fellowship of his people.

Matthias Media has a wide range of excellent resources for Christians to use in the 'gospel growth process'—that is, to facilitate outreach, follow-up, growth and training (see chapter 7).

In listing and recommending resources, we're not for a minute suggesting that simply by running a course or setting up a new program, all your worries will be over. These Bible studies or training courses are not magic bullets; they are frameworks for disciple-making.

For example, the *Just for Starters* set of Bible studies is designed for following up new Christians and helping them become established in the faith. And it's been used for this purpose by tens of thousands of people around the world over the past 20 years. However, it's not *Just for Starters* that does the follow-up. That happens through personal relationship and ministry—through a more mature Christian getting next to a new Christian, meeting regularly with them, sticking with them, praying for them, and sharing their struggles and victories over an extended period of time. It happens, in other words, as one Christian disciples another. What the Bible studies do is improve the quality and efficiency of this process. They provide tested, proven, high-quality biblical material that works through all the important subjects a new Christian needs to think about. And by saving the time of having to devise and write these studies yourself, you are more able to pour your time and energy into personal ministry relationships.

All of the Matthias Media resources operate on this principle. We want to support and promote gospel ministry by providing high-quality, reliable, ready-to-hand tools to do the job. You can browse the full range of our resources at **www.matthiasmedia.com**, but here is a selection of the key ones.

To facilitate outreach

Two Ways to Live is a memorable summary of the gospel that has been used to share the gospel with hundreds of thousands of people around the world. It comes in a range of styles, formats and languages, but each different resource that uses the *Two Ways to Live* framework features the same six-step logical presentation of what the Bible says about Jesus Christ.

For more information, go to **twowaystolive.com**.

To facilitate follow-up

Used by thousands of churches worldwide, *Just for Starters* is widely regarded as *the* Bible study for following up new Christians. The seven studies look at what the Bible teaches on seven fundamental topics: Saved by God, Trusting in God, Living God's way, Listening to God, Talking to God, Meeting with God's family, Meeting the world.

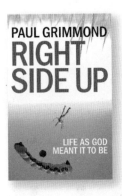

This recent book by Paul Grimmond is especially designed for new Christians, to orient them to the new life that they have embarked upon with Christ. It not only clearly explains the gospel (so that the foundations are solid), but also goes on to discuss the many practical issues and challenges that new believers face. It's a warm-hearted, engaging, exciting read about the adventure of the Christian life, and as such is very helpful as a refresher for longer-serving Christians as well.

To facilitate growth

The basis of all Christian growth is regular feeding from God's word. Matthias Media publishes two series of Bible studies for individuals and small groups.

Pathway Bible Guides: shorter, simpler studies that are easy to digest

Interactive Bible Studies: solid food for growing Christians

Both series focus closely on the passage of Scripture, rather than bouncing too quickly into discussion or application; both seek to read the passage in its context; and both maintain a balance between providing input and direction, and allowing plenty of room for exploration and discovery.

To facilitate training

Our best-known training program is *Two Ways to Live: Know and share the gospel*. This seven-session course teaches participants to know the gospel thoroughly for themselves, and then trains them in how to explain that message clearly and naturally in their own words, using the well-known *Two Ways to Live* framework. With role-plays, DVD and audio input, the course is easy to run and highly effective.

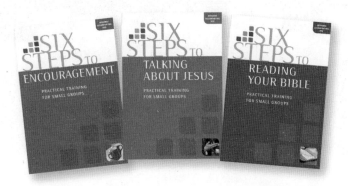

The other main plank in our training resources is the DVD-based Six Steps range, now with three titles in the series. Each one contains simple, straightforward training for every Christian in a basic area of Christian living and ministry:

- *Six Steps to Encouragement*: how to encourage one another with God's word
- *Six Steps to Talking About Jesus*: how to begin to share your faith with others
- *Six Steps to Reading your Bible*: how to dig into God's word for yourself.

These courses are ideal for running in existing small groups as a framework for training people in knowledge, godliness and the ability to serve others.

Colin Marshall talks to Phillip Jensen about MTS training

CM: Can MTS be written up as a system or curriculum?

PJ: Systems never worked for me. I think ministry is caught as much as it is taught. No, it might be more accurate to say that I rationalize my personality the way you rationalize yours. So my rationalization is that ministry is caught as well as taught.

What one individual needs to hear is different from another. I will enthuse someone when I am enthusiastic about something, and I'm usually enthusiastic about new ideas or the latest ideas—things I'm wrestling with. We're training officers, not soldiers, so we need to train in principle rather than in procedure. So it doesn't matter which issue we are talking about, if we can get back to the principle that lies behind it. Then, when our trainees face different issues, they can apply those principles elsewhere. I'm happy to talk about whatever they want to talk about.

CM: What's an example from this week with your trainees?

PJ: I read this week about child-raising and 'warehousing' children. Raising our children as Christians and ministers is an abiding issue. One of my principles is not to follow the fads and fashions of the day in child-raising. Another principle is not to read too many books on the subject, for that only confuses matters. I want to ask: What does the Bible say about raising children?

CM: So you just came across this article in the newspaper and turned it into a training topic. Your juices were stirred so you got your trainees all excited about it in a staff meeting. But how do you know you've covered everything over the two years of MTS?

PJ: I haven't.

CM: But doesn't that leave gaps in the training?

PJ: Yes and no. They're not gaps if you never intended to cover everything. Training is a lifetime thing, and you have to learn to think. You don't learn to think with a closed curriculum. It's about learning to see the world through the Bible's lenses.

CM: So you can start with any topic and get them thinking biblically.

PJ: They need to see the world from the perspective of the gospel and the ministry of the gospel. Then they go to theological college with that framework. So I don't need to teach them a curriculum course in church history, but I do want them to understand who the good guys and the bad guys are, and how history has shaped us to be the way we are. So I'm happy to paint the big picture, knowing that when they get to college they will get the details.

CM: You don't worry about the dates.

PJ: I want engineers (for example) to want to learn history and open their minds. Christianity is very historical.

CM: But as pastors start to train someone as an MTS trainee, they may not have your capacity to just start with a topic and turn it into a training session. Can anyone learn to do that? Do some trainers just need to work through a curriculum?

PJ: I suspect you will be what you will be. Your trainees will grow to be like you, whatever you are like. Yes, we are all different. Trainees and trainers burn with passion about different things. So for some trainers, Reformed theology is what excites them, so they will train their trainees by working through Louis Berkhof. That's all right. The sheep will always grow like the shepherd. So you'll get people coming out who are like that. I could start with Berkhof, but within about three chapters I would get lost or forget or...

CM: ...want to re-write it.

PJ: So I suppose that means there will be a lot of flibbertigibbets coming out of my training—people who can't concentrate for more than a few minutes on one subject!

CM: So if the exact method doesn't matter very much and the personality of the trainer also doesn't matter, what's the bottom line when you're training an apprentice pre-college?

PJ: You're reproducing yourself, really. So you have to make sure that the bit of you that you reproduce is the important bit. You've got to reproduce the gospel; you've got to reproduce godliness. For me, Christian liberty is very important. I don't think you get the gospel right unless you understand Christian liberty. So I don't want them to become like me in terms of liking rugby or cricket or "You've got to do it this way". I want them to become like me in the gospel and in godliness.

CM: I always found it very liberating that you taught us to minister through our own personalities.

PJ: Yes, so you don't have to come and be like Phillip Jensen. That would be awful.

CM: Awful—yep!

PJ: I beg your pardon. I have to put up with this personality all the time. To see lots of little me's all around would be a dreadful experience not just for the world, but also for me. I want Tim Thorburn to be the best Tim Thorburn he can ever be, and Peter Blowes to be the best Peter Blowes he can ever be.[1] That's why (it may be my rationalization) I want them to tell me what subject they want to wrestle through, rather than me telling them they've got to think this or do it that way. That's why I don't want to have a curriculum that tells them these are the things to do. But I think there are people out there who would be really good curriculum teachers and for whom a curriculum would be a great help.

CM: Do you get officers out of curriculum teaching?

PJ: I think less so. The soldiers get trained through the manual. My colleague Mark Charleston, who was in the army, tells me that we are now operating with two different kinds of infantry: infantry and SAS. With the infantry, you put them in the battle and tell them where the enemy is and how to proceed. With the SAS, you drop them down somewhere in the battlefield and tell them the enemy is somewhere within a 360-degree arc around them, and you wish them the best of British luck. The non-manual training will best train the SAS but can be confusing for someone who needs an infantry procedure, someone who can't proceed unless they've got a system. I probably wouldn't be the best trainer for them.

Endnote
1. Tim and Peter were some of Phillip's very first trainees.

 matthiasmedia

Matthias Media is an evangelical publishing ministry that seeks to persuade all Christians of the truth of God's purposes in Jesus Christ as revealed in the Bible, and equip them with high-quality resources, so that by the work of the Holy Spirit they will:

- abandon their lives to the honour and service of Christ in daily holiness and decision-making
- pray constantly in Christ's name for the fruitfulness and growth of his gospel
- speak the Bible's life-changing word whenever and however they can—in the home, in the world and in the fellowship of his people.

It was in 1988 that we first started pursuing this mission, and in God's kindness we now have more than 300 different ministry resources being used all over the world. These resources range from Bible studies and books through to training courses and audio sermons.

To find out more about our large range of very useful resources, and to access samples and free downloads, visit our website:

www.matthiasmedia.com

How to buy our resources

1. Direct from us over the internet:
   – in the US: www.matthiasmedia.com
   – in Australia and the rest of the world: www.matthiasmedia.com.au

2. Direct from us by phone:
   – in the US: 1 866 407 4530
   – in Australia: 1300 051 220
   – international: +61 2 9233 4627

> Register at our website for our **free** regular email update to receive information about the latest new resources, **exclusive special offers**, and free articles to help you grow in your Christian life and ministry.

3. Through a range of outlets in various parts of the world. Visit **www.matthiasmedia.com/contact** for details about recommended retailers in your part of the world, including www.thegoodbook.co.uk in the United Kingdom.

4. Trade enquiries can be addressed to:
   – in the US and Canada: sales@matthiasmedia.com
   – Australia and the rest of the world: sales@matthiasmedia.com.au

MINISTRY TRAINING
STRATEGY

MTS is an independent training ministry, training ministers of the gospel to declare the saving work of Christ to the world. Our focus is to train men and women as faithful and competent Bible teachers who will serve Christ as pastors, evangelists and church-planters. MTS began informally in 1979 on the campus at the University of New South Wales, and in 1992 was established more formally to serve the wider church. We work with ministers across many denominations and specialist ministries, equipping them to train others for the work of the gospel.

Contact details:

Mail: MTS Ltd
          PO Box 978
          Hurstville NSW 2220
          Australia

Email: mts@mts.com.au

Phone: +61-2-9570-5193

To find out more about MTS, and to gain access to the resources and services MTS offers, visit our website:

www.mts.com.au

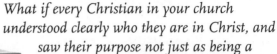

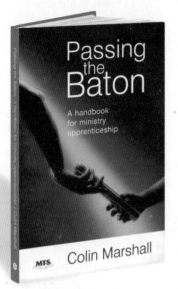

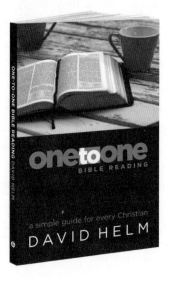